Oct 13

CHRISTIANS IN A CHANGING WORLD

Christians in

A Changing

World

48659

BX
2350.2
.G4

Dennis J. Geaney, O.S.A.

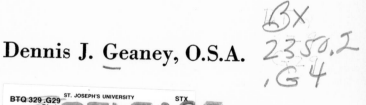

FIDES PUBLISHERS ASSOCIATION, CHICAGO 19, ILL.

Library of Congress Catalog Card Number: 59-7819

Manufactured by American Book-Stratford Press, Inc., New York

Contents

Foreword	Patrick A. O'Boyle, D.D.	vii
Chapter I	Social Change and the Church	3
Chapter II	Social Role and Vocation	10
Chapter III	Change in the Layman's Role	18
Chapter IV	Catholic Laymen in a New Land	26
Chapter V	Changing Parishes	40
Chapter VI	The Fragmented Family	63
Chapter VII	Family Movements	79
Chapter VIII	The Teens and Change	98
Chapter IX	The Downtown Apostolate	113
Chapter X	Spirituality for the Laity	134
Chapter XI	A View of the Apostolate	148
Chapter XII	The Priesthood Amidst Change	161

ACKNOWLEDGMENTS

The author wishes to acknowledge his indebtedness to the Very Rev. George G. Higgins, for inviting him to lecture at the Institute of Social Action for Priests and Seminarians during the summer sessions of Catholic University. This book grew out of those courses. The author is likewise indebted to the following, who graciously read and criticized parts of the manuscript: Rt. Rev. John Tracey Ellis, Rev. Bernard G. Murchland, C.S.C., Rev. Godfrey Diekmann, O.S.B., Rev. Shawn Sheehan, Rev. Walter Imbiorski, Mr. Edward Marciniak, Mr. John McCudden, Dr. Ruth Shonle Cavan, and Mrs. Mary Carroll Divina. He is particularly indebted to Mrs. Catherine Smith for the typing. The editors of *Worship, Ave Maria, Commonweal,* and *Today* graciously permitted the use of articles previously published in those publications.

Foreword

One of the most fascinating characteristics of the Church of Christ is her adaptability. True to our Lord's comparison of her to a householder who brings forth from his treasury new things and old, the Church has continually presented her changeless treasures to a changing world in ways adapted to the needs of that world. While ever remaining essentially the same, she has never feared to shed that which has become ineffective and take up new weapons, adopt new measures to meet new situations. The history of the Church is the history of her marvellous adaptability.

Every age has presented a challenge, and the Church in every age has met that challenge with imagination and daring which have often been nothing less than heroic. At the very beginning the challenge required a bold break with the forms of the old Judaism. Later it required an immersion into the culture of

Rome. At another time it required a fearless reformation of herself in answer to the so-called Reformation of the Protestants. And today, when the world is changing at a pace hitherto unheard of, once again the Church is meeting the challenge. Once again she is giving evidence of her eternal youth.

Change does not come easily to many of us. We feel safe and secure with what is familiar. We do not relish the thought of abandoning ideas and methods which served us well in the past. This reluctance to change is understandable, but we must not let it blind us to the fact that change has already taken place all around us and that we must adapt ourselves to it. The children of the Church must grow with the Church. The members of the Body of Christ must be alert to the promptings of the Holy Spirit, Who quickens that Body. But first of all they must open their eyes to the world about them. They must see it not as it used to be, but as it is.

What Father Geaney has done for us in this book is to help us to open our eyes. The world we live in, he points out, is a different sort of place than the world we used to know. Our homes and neighborhoods are different. Our cities are different. Step by step he analyzes the institutions of modern life. But, not content with mere analysis, Father Geaney also outlines the means of apostolic formation which are providentially at hand and presents a challenge which may stimulate Catholics in all walks of life to try new experiments.

One of the most obvious features of the Church in the twentieth century is, as Father Geaney points out, the awakening of the laity to a realization of their role in her mission. Consequently, he has a great deal to say about the lay apostolate. But, as he also points out, priests and people must work together in restoring all things in Christ. Therefore, he also examines the role of the priest in the modern world.

Here, then, we have food for thought for both laymen and priests. It is my hope and prayer that it will be widely read and pondered. May it stimulate us all, priests and people, to a deeper realization of and greater dedication to our glorious common work—the restoration of all things in Christ.

✚ PATRICK A. O'BOYLE
Archbishop of Washington

Washington, D. C.
December 4, 1958

CHRISTIANS IN A CHANGING WORLD

CHAPTER I

Social Change and the Church

T HE CHRISTIAN can never be accused of leading a double life because he lives in two worlds. He is immersed in the temporal affairs of men but always with an awareness that he is at the same time in God's eternal presence. The true Christian lives a really human life but this life is divinized by another life, the God-life in his soul. St. Cyril of Alexandria uses the comparison of a piece of iron put into the fire; the iron retains its own nature, but absorbs the heat of the fire and takes on, as it were, the qualities of the fire itself. So, too, our human nature is transformed by the divine life dwelling in us.

Although the Christian shares life with Christ even while on earth, this cannot relieve him from a commitment to earthly life. Nor can his concern for this world make him less concerned with the eternal. The Christian belongs to this world completely. He does not reject his times. Without forfeiting and

3

prejudicing his citizenship in the human community, he possesses the credentials for membership in the heavenly community. It would be a violation of the Christian's relation to the world to portray him suspended between heaven and earth. If a symbol for his position is needed, it will have to be one that anchors him in both worlds at once.

With mankind eternity issues from the womb of time. Since time bears eternity and without time there is for us no eternity, time is already, in some sense, eternity. For this reason, everything one does has eternal reverberations. If the hairs of one's head are numbered, of how much more eternal significance are the human relationships which constitute the inner meaning of human life and the basis of salvation. Our Lord's description of the judgment scene deals exclusively with our response to human situations or temporal concerns: "I was hungry . . . thirsty . . . a stranger . . . naked . . . sick and in prison . . . " Our Lord made no attempt at a complete enumeration of the associations we have with people in daily life. He merely pointed out kinds of temporal actions that are important enough to include or exclude us from His eternal friendship. He was offering us keys to the Kingdom—keys that are cut from the metal of living contacts with others.

Since our Blessed Lord was the Son of God, we think of Him as timeless. And so He was. But He was also a man of time. Everything about Him suggested His timeliness. He lived in a certain section of a certain country. He had parents and relatives whose genealogies we can trace. He wore a garb that dated Him. He spoke a dialect that localized Him. He followed religious customs that committed Him to a particular religion. His hands had the hardness of a craftsman. His feet were toughened by Palestinian roads. He made no effort to escape this particularization, this identity, this relationship with histori-

The Church is immutable because it is anchored to eternal truth and has the promise that it will never be loosed from its mooring. Dictators and dynasties will rise and fall, but the Church will remain.

But this is only one view of the Church; it is one side of the coin. The recent sweeping changes in the Eucharistic fast serve as one example of what is immutable and what is changing in the Church. The late Pope Pius XII, seeing the far reaching sociological changes in our society that made frequent reception of the Eucharist difficult and morning Mass sometimes impossible, with a single stroke cut away the fasting regulations of centuries. Speaking for the Holy Father, Cardinal Ottaviani said, "The Sovereign Pontiff paternally concerned with the salvation of souls . . . wished to give to the faithful with these new rules on afternoon Mass and Eucharistic fast a broader possibility of assisting at the Sacrifice of the Mass and of approaching the Eucharistic table, in order to strengthen themselves in the life of grace . . . The Church, justly severe and inflexible where doctrinal principles are concerned, knows nevertheless how to harmonize everything that is of ecclesiastical discipline with the circumstances of the times."

The Church is Christ's permanent incarnation—always taking new flesh, always close to its times, immersed in human concerns while transcending them. Change within the Church must always be made in the spirit of obedience. It is not the obedience of the lethargic who sit and wait for orders before moving. It is the obedience and docility of the pioneer who with boldness and creative initiative makes his thrust into the unknown and presents his findings to authority for approval before another thrust is made.

CHAPTER II

Social Role and Vocation

Louis MARTIN, as a young Frenchman, set out to apply for admission to the great monastery of St. Bernard. Refused because he did not know enough Latin, he was advised to acquire more and apply later. He went back to his native town and became a watchmaker. In time, he met Zelie Guerin, who had given up thoughts of the cloister and wanted a line of sons who would be missionary priests. Their marriage was blessed not with missionary priests but cloistered nuns, one of whom became a canonized saint, Thérèse of Lisieux, the Little Flower.

Because Louis and Zelie gave up the idea of the religious life, could we rightly say they had no vocation? The word "vocation" in Catholic circles is often used without a qualifying adjective and used exclusively in reference to special vocations such as the priesthood and the religious life. "Fostering vocations," means cooperating with God in the development of the priestly or religious callings. "Father, I think the boy has a vocation," means only one thing in Catholic circles. A vocation director in a Catholic school usually is a person whose job is to recruit for this special type of vocation.

A case can be made for this unqualified use of "vocation." The priestly and religious vocations are marked by either a sacramental character or a public religious profession. Each marks a radical choice that, in the case of the priest, lasts even after death. There is a formal acceptance by the Church and a pronounced departure from the common modes of life. The answer to the call is marked by the wearing of a distinctive garb and, in the case of sisters, a change of names as well. The investiture ceremony or the ordination rites, the garb and manner of life, keep alive the idea of Christian vocation in the layman's mind. While he is not called to embrace this life, he is reminded by its very existence of the Christian concept of a divine mission, of a total commitment to Christ.

There is no doubt that a special appeal must be made today by priests and religious, and judicious encouragement given by parents, to fill the ranks of the diocesan priests and of religious communities. But what about the vast majority who have no calling to this special and highest vocation. Do these have a calling to anything? Does it matter to God what they do? We know He has a plan for their eternal salvation, but does He through His Providence call them to a particular vocation? Is there any relation between their social roles and the notion of vocation? The matter seems worth probing.

The theology of the priestly vocation gives a clue to the theology of the lay vocation. Near the turn of the century, a theological controversy arose over the requirements for a priestly vocation. St. Pius X settled it with the same finality that he used in settling the problem of frequent and early communion.

Through his secretary, Cardinal Del Val, he wrote: "Nothing more is required in the candidate in order that he may be rightly called by the bishop, than a right intention together with a fitness placed in those gifts of nature and grace and confirmed by that probity of life and sufficiency of learning, which furnish a well-founded hope that he may be able to discharge properly the duties of the priesthood and to fulfill holily its obligations. . . ."

Briefly, what St. Pius said was that the candidate need not wait for parted tongues of fire to appear over his head. What is required, simply, is that along with the bishop's call there is a desire and fitness for the office. If there is a desire and fitness and no bishop who will ordain him, the candidate has no vocation. An American theologian, Monsignor William O'Connor, concludes from this that *all* vocations will be found to be a "providential meeting of a suitably disposed nature with the right opportunity for doing some good." Both the layman and the priest must have the natural endowment, the desire to do the work, and the opportunity to do it. In both cases, there is no need for a special act of God to make the call heard. The decision is arrived at by a study of our nature, our interests, and the opportunities to express our nature and follow our interests. The man who likes to write but because of poor craftsmanship and lack of perception cannot convince publishers that his work is worthy of publication has obviously not been called to be a journalist. He is like the seminarian who is advised to leave the seminary.

If a person wants to ask himself what his vocation is, he must look realistically at his nature. Basically, what God asks of each of us is that we fulfill our nature. We fulfill our nature when we do what it inclines us to do. The girl who has a desire to express sympathy and care for the sick and enjoys doing this work would be fulfilling her nature as a nurse. When the circumstances are such that she has the opportunity to fulfill her nature as a way of life, we say that she is called to the nursing profession. Nursing is her vocation.

When a Christian begins to examine his life on the subject of vocations, he will ordinarily find that he likes the type of work he is doing. The desire, the fulfilling of his nature, and the opportunity are present. Or, he may be doing a work for which he is suited, but always has the desire to do something different. When the opportunity for the latter is lacking, the present work he is doing must be seen as a providential calling which we call a vocation.

In our moments of meditation after Communion or during a retreat, or simply after a talk on the urgency of the lay apostolate we may be fired up with zeal. We want to win the world for Christ. We imagine ourselves on a charger like Saul on the way to Damascus. We want to change the world radically and bring it into conformity with Christ's designs. Changing the world is not simply a matter of enthusiasm, but also one of sober, penetrating analysis and plodding effort until the job is done. Unless we have a mature view on how these objectives can be accomplished in our highly organized society, we shall be filling Leacock's description of the man mounting his horse and galloping off in all directions. The concept of vocation must be studied in terms of what the sociologist calls social roles. These are simply customary ways of carrying out social functions. In analyzing the role of the teacher in society, we would examine, besides his prescribed duties, his relationship to the student, to the parent, to the school, and to the community. The role, briefly, is the sum total expected of a person who performs this function in society. We learn how to play roles from society itself. We unconsciously assimilate the attitudes and habits of mind and body that go with the roles.

If I have an ample wardrobe, packing a suitcase for a trip calls for decisions. What will I be doing on the trip? Will there be formal affairs? Will there be sports affairs such as swimming, fishing, or golfing? Will there be manual labor to be done? For each of the roles I will play on the trip, there is a special attire that society considers fitting. Wardrobes describe roles.

We play many parts in life simultaneously. A man enters his plant each morning wearing the distinctive garb of the business man or the tool and die maker. While at work he speaks the language or the jargon of the group. It may be formal or it may be vulgar and, in either case, different from the language of the family circle.

At five o'clock, the efficient young executive who has been on his dignity all day may close his office door and open the door of the cocktail bar. Behind this door he is the relaxed, hail-fellow well-met, back-slapping buddy to his cronies. Later, when he sits behind the wheel of his car and fights his way through traffic, this gentle Christian spirit may become a can-tankerous, cussing motorist. In his own home, he faces a dif-ferent set of relationships and assumes different roles. No longer is he the boss, the fellow worker, the buddy, the motorist. He now plays the roles of husband to his wife, and father to his children.

There are also other roles he plays: He is a neighbor to the man next door; he is a taxpayer to the local government; he is a voter to the mayor, governor and president; he is a customer at the local store, a client to the lawyer, a patient to the doc-tor, a reader to the journalist. Although we all play multiple roles, there is usually a dominant role by which people neatly classify us as banker, priest, or housewife. Although our other roles are important, this one is a convenient point of reference for others for placing us in a category.

Probably the best vantage point for the Christian to study change and its effects on the human personality is within the framework of roles. If the world is to reflect the justice and charity of Christ, the roles through which the acts of justice and charity are performed must be Christianized. If the roles are Christian in orientation they become beacons that lead new generations to perform their roles in a Christian way.

Society is a network of social institutions, such as business, recreation, education, the family and the Church; the institution in turn is a network of social roles. It is in changing these social roles that we change institutions and thus change the world. To fulfill the motto of St. Pius X, "To restore all things in Christ," means concretely to restore the social roles we play. A college sophomore may not see how he can change the educational system when he is struggling to pass exams, but he may be challenged to play his student role more in conformity with the Gospel by doing collateral reading for today's and tomorrow's classes. The Gospel must ultimately live in the roles we play.

Christ has a stake in role playing. The Incarnation will never be complete from our point of view until each person plays his roles in a Christian way. The social roles get to the heart of Christian reform. The Sermon on the Mount must be applied to particular circumstances and modes of acting. Pius XII was very much aware of approaching the Christian message from the vantage point of roles. When a group of engineers, doctors, laborers, or cyclists came to him for an audience, he did not talk about Christianity in general; he told them about their science or their profession and how that chief role was related to the Christian message.

Our vocation corresponds to our social role. Our major social function may be that of a lawyer or housewife, and so this may be our primary vocation. The concept of primary vocation must not be pushed too far, and the concept of major social role must not be considered our sole function in life, lest we neglect many other facets of the life to which God calls us. As one theologian has said: "The offers of Divine Providence are several or even many . . . and we may say of every good that we do, that we had the vocation to do it. . . ."

What we are doing is examining our sociological role in the light of God's loving and wise Providence. This reflection or re-assessment will not ordinarily result in changing the major roles of our life. What it should do is to help us see these roles in reference to the Divine Plan. We should see new implications and fresh opportunities to link our lives with the saving work of Christ's Mystical Body.

We should, therefore, see in our social role the will of God, that is, our vocation, and have the desire to conform to it and be obedient to this calling as Christ conformed to the will of His Father and was obedient unto the death of the Cross. If a person is a shoemaker, he will try to make better shoes; or if he is a shoe salesman, he will be interested in really satisfied customers. In the case of the shoemaker, he will look upon his last as a key to heaven and the shoe salesman will see his shop as the foyer of the Heavenly Kingdom.

A very practical problem arises when a person has many talents and a keen sense of mission or vocation. He wants to restore all things to Christ, but finds himself limited by the hours of the day and the demands of nature for food and rest. He wants to make a contribution to his professional association or trade union; leaders of civic projects and political party chieftains call upon him for his services and he listens to their appeals with a Christian awareness that these aspects of life, too, belong to Christ. Parish organizations all vie for his active membership; if he makes a notable contribution in civic or parish organizations, the city-wide and diocesan-wide Catholic organizations will put his generosity to a further test.

Then there are the demands of the family. He has a wife to love, storm windows to put up, walks to shovel, grass to cut, tots to play with, grade-schoolers to help or encourage with their homework, plus time merely to be in the presence of the family so that all know what it is like to have a father in the house.

In this case, it is not a question of an opportunity being wanting, but of too many opportunities and a nature so developed that it is adaptable to a multiplicity of roles. Obviously, a choice has to be made. Presuming his major occupational vocation has been determined, on what basis will he pick and choose among the numerous demands upon his time? The wisdom of Solomon is needed. Since no two people have the same potentialities or the same circumstances of life, no two people can be expected to make the same choices.

A person's choice will be made on the basis of his unique talents and the need which he can fulfill in a way that no other person can. After the choice has been intelligently and prayerfully made, the person must see it as a vocation, without a sigh of regret for the many things that he is capable of doing, but which circumstances have proved him not called to.

CHAPTER III

Change in the Layman's Role

MISSIONARY DEPARTURE CEREMONIES are not uncommon. The scene is usually a church, the presiding prelate a bishop or a provincial. Included in the ritual is the receiving of a letter assigning the missionary to a particular mission territory; and a cross is given the modern crusader to remind him that he is to follow in the footsteps of his Master, Jesus Christ.

This is commonplace and makes no headlines in Catholic newspapers. What has made such events first-page news recently is not, as in one case, that a Cardinal presided, but that seventeen laymen were departing for the missions. An osteopathic physician, a registered nurse, a printer, an engraver, a commercial artist, a librarian, and a commercial pilot were included in this group of skilled technicians. These people with their technical competence were to place themselves in the service of a local bishop in a missionary territory.

Another item in a Catholic paper was the picture of an Archbishop with sixteen graduates of a Catholic women's college who volunteered for assignment in understaffed schools in remote parts of this country. This brought to fifty-seven the number of graduates from this school who had joined the school's lay apostolate program.

These two random items from the West and East Coasts point to a significant trend in the Church today. The increasing importance of the layman in the Church is attested by the two World Congresses of the lay apostolate held in Rome in this decade. The first was in 1951, the second in 1957. Equally revealing was the increased participation of the United States in the second Congress over the first. The first American delegation numbered twenty-two, representing about seven national organizations. At the 1957 Congress, the United States was represented by about 125 delegates representing twenty-six national organizations.

There is no doubt that the Church is throwing its full weight behind the lay apostolate. It is the demand of the times, the very urgency of the hour, which presses the Church to urge the laity into combat. The Church must choose either a mobilization of the laity or a gradual withdrawal of the Church's influence among men everywhere. One would gather from papal documents of the past twenty-five years that the lay apostolate is simply an "either—or" proposition.

It seems that everyone who writes on the subject insists that the lay apostolate is a new label for something as old as the Church. For evidence, they offer the writings of St. Paul. In one Epistle he mentions the names of thirty lay helpers. There were also laymen among the Church Fathers. When the subject of the restoration of deacons for missionary areas was presented to the 1956 Liturgical Congress in Assisi, the plea was based on the early tradition of the Church. The Apostles ordained deacons to care for temporal needs so that the priests would be free for the ministry of the Word.

What has happened to this vital role of the laymen since the era of the Fathers? While it is true that the layman has always had a share in the mission of the Church, between the fourth and the twentieth centuries active lay participation in the work of the Church was on retreat. During the Middle Ages, due to political circumstances, the roles of Church and state, priest and layman, were not clearly distinguished; the result was that, to a large degree, the clerical side of the Church absorbed the lay. A cursory glance at the history of the Mass shows what happened to liturgical participation by the laity. Silence replaced song. The altar boys' responses were substituted for the people's. The offertory procession gave way to the collection. Holy Communion became the daily Bread of an elite instead of all. The laity were left without a single "Amen"; they were reduced to passive, paying members.

The restoration and adaptation of the lay vocation in our times has resulted from political conditions as much as from theological tracts or papal exhortations. From the statistician's point of view, the Church is losing ground. The world is witnessing a population explosion, particularly in Asia, where the Church is numerically weakest. While the number of priests increases each year, the increase in the number of people is proportionately greater. On the local level pastors are forced increasingly to consider the possibilities of lay assistance. The bishop informs a pastor that no assistant is available for his burgeoning parish; Mother Provincial informs him that there is no possibility of adding another sister in the Fall.

If bishops in long established dioceses of this country are hard put to find priests for the new parishes in the mushrooming suburbs, imagine the problem of the mission country or the Catholic continent of South America, where the shortage was acute even before the population boom. In this country people will be lost to the Church in areas where real estate developers have moved in thousands of families almost overnight, leaving the Church no time to adjust to the problem.

Every ten years, on the basis of the United States Census Report, the congressional districts are redivided to give a more proportionate representation to the people. It is hardly conceivable that the Pope or the American hierarchy will devise a similar system to adjust to such conditions as the dislocation of clergy brought about by the lack of vocations in certain areas, a mobile laity settling in boom states, and the population bursts. However, something is being done in this regard by Archbishop Ritter, who sent St. Louis priests to South America, and by Cardinal Cushing, who has generously lent priests to under-staffed dioceses around the country and more recently established a society of diocesan missionary priests for South America.

The dislocation must not be confused with the fundamental problem of shortage. The latter must be viewed as something which will endure and will demand long-range planning. Besides the encouragement of vocations to the clerical and religious states, there must be an effort to enlist the layman in work that will free the priest for his purely spiritual tasks. In the past, priests have performed such roles as recreational director, substitute school-janitor and sexton, chauffeur for vacation schools, fund-raiser, bookkeeper, architect. These are tasks for which there should be an abundance of lay volunteers.

Even in his own tasks, the priest needs lay helpers. The priests of large, under-staffed parishes can hardly arrange time to visit all the families, Catholic and non-Catholic, in the parish.

The fact is that, in visiting Protestants, the layman may be a more effective link than the priest. Lay people have shown great enthusiasm and have done superb work for the Church when enlisted for such purposes.

There is no mystery in the fact that the current of life does not flow through the rectory door. The people inside dress differently, live a peculiar form of family life, and do not follow the ordinary pursuits of the men in the neighborhood. The rectory is not a family residence in the ordinary sense of the term. It is a place where one goes to arrange for a baptism, a marriage or a burial service. People may ring the doorbell occasionally when they are at their wits' end to know what to do with a straying partner or an alcoholic member of the family, but rarely do they come to the rectory to find how the truths of Christ have relevance to the economic, political, recreational, and educational areas of life.

The lay apostolate is the answer. The apostolate is not lay people on their own without the inspiration of the priest; nor is it the priest calling the plays and telling the lay people what to do. The pastor who ruled his immigrant flock with an iron hand while he lovingly protected them from the exploitations of the city slicker must change with the times. Changing gears for older priests is not easy; and for that matter, I suppose, the majority of the laity would just as soon have things the way they are. There is, however, an ever growing number of priests and lay people sensitive to the Church's mission in our times and sufficiently restless to desire a change. The dawning age of the laity sees the pastor and the parishioner as a partnership, with the pastor having the controlling vote. The enlightened pastor's slogan is "Teamwork Does It."

The layman helping the pastor carry out his apostolate is an important part of the lay apostolate. Without this lay effort, the saving work of Christ's Church will be hampered. There is, however, another and wider area for the lay apostolate. It is lay life itself for which the layman, and not the priest, has a primary responsibility. One might conceive of the lay role of priest's helper being dispensed with or mitigated by an increase in religious vocations, but no increase in the number of priests can lessen the layman's importance in the world of work, the family, recreation, political life.

The "Employees Only" sign over the entrance to the industrial world reminds the priest that here he is an intruder or at best a guest, but never a citizen. Inside, the layman is supreme. This is his citadel. Here he makes decisions in his own right. Yet this industrial world belongs to Christ and must be restored to Him. It must reflect His justice, truth and love. In a sense, it must be "redeemed."

Historically, this problem was ushered in with the industrial era and the rise of democracy. This was the time when the Church was at its weakest, a time when the teachings of Karl Marx were going unchallenged and were stealing the initiative from the Church. Education in the West, once under control of the Church through the medieval university, was becoming mass education, taking place, to an ever greater degree, outside the sphere of the Church's influence. Tremendous advances in the social and technical sciences were being made without the guiding presence of the Church and with only a token contribution from it. To be added to this litany of nineteenth-century losses in influence, is the population explosion of the twentieth century; now the Church must cope with a rising tide of peoples and newly felt national aspirations at a time when it is clerically understaffed in some of the older Catholic countries.

This new society has come into existence without an adequate effort to relate its conditions to man's temporal and eternal destiny through the disciplines of philosophy and theology; generally speaking, Catholic theology has been removed from the university and relegated to the learned obscurity of the seminary. Today the world recognizes the legitimate autonomy of this lay society, but fails to see that it must be animated by the spirit of Christ.

The hierarchical Church has no competence or mission to direct the affairs of the temporal order, but it does have a mission to witness to truth and justice. The teaching Church proposes no solutions to technical problems; it merely pleads that the solutions be in conformity with man's nature. The spiritual and temporal orders can be bridged only by lay people, who have membership in Christ's Mystical Body and citizenship in this world. People who can legitimately pass the "Employees Only" sign, whether in a factory, a brokerage house, a TV station, or a governmental office, form what Pius XII called, "the front ranks of the Church." It is this aspect of the layman's role in the Church that is new. Because the layman's role in the world changed, his role in the Church demanded re-defining.

The Church is a living organism. It has its seasons of growth and decline, its springs and its winters. The incessant calls of Pius XI and Pius XII to the work of the lay apostolate have been a fresh breath of the Spirit, "who blows where He wills." Today is another springtime of the Church. There is a notable progression of thought on the lay apostolate from one Pope to the next. What was remarkable about Pius XII's approach was that it called all. He blessed movements and approved organizations, but he did not establish a hierarchy of importance among them, nor did he offer patterns to be imitated. He did not dictate the structure of these organizations, nor did he require close consultation with their representatives as to their goals. This method left the door open for individual initiative, and adaptation to varied local needs. Likewise, it offered flexibility to rapidly changing social needs.

While Pius XII encouraged a variety of forms of organized lay activity, he also appealed for an apostolate of laymen outside the structure of the organized lay apostolate—for what Monsignor Pavan calls "the apostolate of animation."

This is how Monsignor Pavan described Pius XII's concern for this work of animation: "Throughout his pontificate his voice has rung out and continues to ring out unceasingly—with clear, warning tone, and often with dramatic accent, urging the presence of a lifegiving leaven in the temporal structures of our civilization; urging it also for the reason that, without this leaven, modern civilization would be doomed to catastrophe; atomic energy, for instance, instead of being used for civil purposes, would finally be attributed to works of destruction and death and would bring about the end of the human family."

By confirmation, every layman is given a mandate for the apostolate of animation. He is expected to proceed on his own initiative and responsibility. His successes bring triumph to the Church, his failures and shortcomings remain his own. While the apostolate of animation advances on its own initiative, it is bound to orthodoxy; the layman must continually seek to be informed and guided by Church teaching. Thus he neither forfeits his lay status, nor withdraws from vital communion with the Church.

Many books and many articles have been written on the lay apostolate. There will be many more forthcoming. This is a healthy sign that the laity are on the march. Their armor is not swords and shields, but Christ's love and truth; their goal, not a Holy Land, but the modern world's vast network of human relations, as well as all its academic, scientific, and technical endeavors.

CHAPTER IV

Catholic Laymen in a New Land

T HE CHURCH IN AMERICA is a monument to the principle of accommodation or adaptation. Our country was settled by people who cast their lot with change. It was through bloody change that we overthrew our masters and established a nation. Catholics settling in the country embraced change and sought to reconcile the Church—which, to her enemies, seemed to be a tradition-ridden relic of the Old World—with the spirit of adaptability. The American Catholic today finds an excellent opportunity and a healthy challenge to live the Christian life in the world, and freely continue the worship of the Church of his fathers.

At the turn of the nineteenth century, the Church was blessed with the leadership of Bishops Carroll and England, both of whom grasped the problem of domesticating a foreign Church at a time when the descendants of the Pilgrims were losing their identity and becoming Yankees and Americans. At the time of the American Revolution Catholics were a tiny but respected minority. A century later, at the turn of the twentieth century, the typical American Catholic was no longer the Maryland Catholic gentleman who was esteemed for his plantation holdings. Something had happened during the century. The wide brimmed hat and the easy southern manners gave way to the miner's cap and the heavy foreign accent.

Despite the fact that these later immigrants built our subways and railroads with their back-breaking labor, they were in the eyes of the Yankees and early settlers Europe's unwanted and unwashed. Earlier in the century riots in Boston and Philadelphia protested their presence. Like tidal waves, the immigrants were washing upon our shores in unprecedented numbers with each decade surpassing the previous in number until 1910. It was during this era that we had the leadership of Cardinal Gibbons and Archbishop Ireland. With their European background, both men knew that the immigrants could not retain their Old World customs for long. They knew that if the Church in America was to make a contribution to American life, its members must become fully Americanized.

Their stand was opposed by German Catholics in the Mid-West under the leadership of Peter Cahensly. This group requested the Holy See to appoint bishops according to nationality, the number for each nationality being based on population figures. The argument had its merits. Since the parish was a social unit as well as a religious center, the Germans might choose not to worship at all rather than worship with Irish immigrants—and vice-versa. The main question was, how fast should the Americanizing process proceed? Both sides argued that the Church would be the loser if the other side's position

were upheld. Ultimately, the Gibbons-Ireland school of no-de-
lay-in-integration prevailed.

Cardinal Gibbons has the distinction of being one of the first
Church dignitaries in the United States to espouse the cause of a
labor organization. When this country's first labor movement,
the Knights of Labor, was condemned by the Church as a secret
organization, Gibbons sailed to Rome and successfully pleaded
the cause of the Knights. Thus, the Church in the United States,
as early as 1886, had made common cause with the working
man in his organizational efforts.

Gibbons was backing a new type of union organized according to function in the industrial world, as compared to the
European unions, which were primarily political and religious in
orientation. Traditionally, the Holy See had favored the religious
union, since the latter sought to protect its members' faith. In
this country, the hierarchy, following the lead of Gibbons, has
wholeheartedly endorsed the "neutral" union, which is the basic
concept of the American labor movement.

Labor Day became a holiday some seventy years ago. A
pioneer labor leader, Peter J. McGuire, was its chief advocate.
He wanted a labor holiday that would recognize the dignity of
work, emphasize just rewards for labor's dignity and activity,
and proclaim full partnership of labor in economic life. The
American labor movement chose a September date rather than
the Communists' May 1. American Catholics want to make
their holidays holydays. As a result, on Labor Day across the
country many of our cathedrals and parishes have a Labor Day
Mass that brings together Catholics from the ranks of labor
and management who bring to the altar the workaday life of
mankind. Pius XII cooperated by granting a petition from a
number of American archbishops and permitting American

churches to celebrate the feast of St. Joseph the Worker on Labor Day.

Thanksgiving Day is distinctly American and Protestant in origin. It was established by the New England Pilgrims long before Catholics had an audible voice in this country. After the Pilgrim days, Thanksgiving became part of American living but retained its religious overtones. American Catholics are integrating Thanksgiving Day into American life as they have done with Labor Day. Throughout the nation Catholics participate in a Thanksgiving Day clothing collection, bringing used clothes to the parish hall for distribution to the needy peoples of the world. In 1956, sixteen million pounds were shipped.

American Catholics are taking this secular feast one step further by linking it with the liturgy. The Bishop of the author's diocese wrote to his clergy as follows: "For Catholics the proper observance of Thanksgiving Day is assisting at the Holy Sacrifice of the Mass and receiving Holy Communion. I trust that pastors will arrange to have Mass at a convenient hour on that day, and will encourage the faithful to attend and to receive our Blessed Lord. A display of the fruits of the land near the altar, and blessing the same, might well impress upon the minds of all the continued blessings of God upon our diocese."

Another way in which the Church is adapting herself to change, in this country as well as elsewhere, is in a more liberal use of the vernacular in the liturgy. As early as 1787 Bishop John Carroll wrote: "The great part of our congregations must be utterly ignorant of the meaning and sense of the public offices of the Church. It may have been prudent, for aught I know, to refuse a compliance in this instance with the insulting and reproachful demands of the first reformers; but to continue the practice of the Latin liturgy in the present state of things must be owing either to chimerical fears of innovation or to indolence and inattention in the first pastors of the national Churches in not joining to solicit or indeed ordain this necessary alteration."

The pressure for more vernacular in the liturgy is not coming from the Catholic countries like Italy where, in spite of the permission of Pope Leo XIII to recite the prayers after Mass in the vernacular, they are still said in Latin, and where the reading of the Epistle and Gospel of the Sunday Mass in Italian is the exception. It is from the countries where Catholics are surrounded with vernacularist Protestant neighbors that the pleas come to the Vatican for a greater use of the mother tongue in the liturgy.

This does not mean Catholics are becoming Protestants or Protestants are becoming Catholics. It only means that we can learn from each other and take from each other things that help us worship in our own way. It is the responsibility of authority within the Church to keep the response to social change within the bounds of orthodoxy.

In Church-State relations this country made a fresh start with its Constitution, which gave equal freedom to all religions. Catholics have accepted and defended this equal status as the only practical solution to a religiously pluralistic society. Actually what appeared as a concession or a permissive approach has turned out to be a positive boon to the Catholic Church. The Church has neither the special protection of the State nor the domination or stranglehold that goes with patronage. In this delicate area, the Church in America has adjusted to the contemporary scene without sacrifice of principle.

It seems a valid conclusion from these examples that the greatness of the Catholic Church in the United States lies in its ability to accommodate itself to the highest ideals of the American people without sacrificing one iota of doctrinal integrity.

The layman during the immigration period

Against this background of religious freedom and the valid use of the missionary principle of adaptation, we approach the subject of the layman's status in the Church during the immigration era. The year 1889 marked the centennial of the establishment of the American hierarchy. To celebrate the occasion a group of outstanding Catholic laymen petitioned Cardinal Gibbons to grant permission for a Catholic lay congress in conjunction with the centennial celebration at Baltimore. The Cardinal gave his consent reluctantly and assigned a committee of six bishops to read in advance the speeches that would be given at the Congress. There were others with misgivings. Archbishop Kenrick refused to be present because the event was a "mixed affair." Contrary to the forebodings, the Congress was a success and stimulated the laity. A second Congress was held in Chicago in 1893, again with some misgivings. In spite of the high level of the papers, and the timely questions they raised, the times were not propitious for lay initiative and this European-style Congress came to an end. These lay congresses must be seen in their historical setting and not be considered representative of the early American Church or the present lay effort, which incorporates into its programs an impressive number of conventions and national meetings.

In 1789, when the Catholic hierarchy was established with the appointment of Father John Carroll as bishop, a healthy relationship existed between priest and laity. This relationship was different from the one in Europe, where there was a deep cleavage between priest and people. The frontier spirit demanded a cooperative relationship in the face of almost insurmountable tasks. Before John Carroll died, however, he had on his hands a problem that was to harass his successors for many decades and throw a cloud of suspicion over any attempt of the laity to play an active role in the life of the Church. This was the evil of trusteeism. Trusteeism was an attack upon the authority of the Bishop. In some of the Eastern cities, notably Philadelphia, lay boards or trustees of the parish assumed the financial responsibilities of the parish and with it claimed that the appointment or dismissal of parish priests rested with them and not the Bishop. The principle was also applied to schools and charitable institutions. The pattern was that of American Protestant church government. Trusteeism had to be fought like a heresy, but with great prudence lest there be a schism. It was finally brought to an end by the growing effectiveness of episcopal authority through the Baltimore Councils and the tidal wave of native bigotry which forced Catholics to close ranks before the common foe. With the burial of trusteeism went something good as well as something bad. To have lay people in charge of the temporal affairs in order to free the priest for this spiritual ministry, is sound theory and practice. In suppressing the abuse we were forced to the extreme of denying the laity any part in the temporal administration of Church affairs. This turn of events was not particularly resented by the laity, who were increasingly immigrant in composition. They had their own problems of adjustment to cope with, such as economic insecurity, a foreign language, and nationality barriers. For the most part, they were satisfied with being ministered to, making substantial financial contributions to our school system and supplying the candidates for the novitiates and seminaries.

In stressing the absence of national Catholic congresses and the era of trusteeism, Dr. Henry J. Browne, an historian of the American Church, warns us to beware lest we fail to credit the laity with their share in the early foundations of our Catholic educational system and the Catholic press. It may surprise priests and people who look with dismay upon the rising number of laity on our Catholic school faculties that in the Archdiocese of Baltimore, between 1865 and 1900, twenty-seven new schools were opened of which fifteen were staffed by lay people. Also, the first central Catholic high school began in 1890 in Philadelphia with two priests and eighteen laymen. In 1957 only five dioceses had lay people on their diocesan school board with the Archdiocese of New Orleans achieving the remarkable balance of eight priests and eight laymen (four men and four women).

Today, our Catholic Press almost without exception is clerically owned and with some notable exceptions is clerically edited. We associate the Catholic Press with the clerical side of the Church. The early Catholic Press, on the contrary, had a large core of free-wheeling, hard-hitting lay editors. It was in large part independently owned and not run as a diocesan enterprise as is the case in England today. Among these lay publicists were Orestes Brownson, John Gilmary Shea, James A. McMaster and John Boyle O'Reilly. While there is no evidence currently that the bishops intend to relinquish control of the diocesan papers, there is evidence of a growing maturity in dealing with problems other than those in which the Church is involved as a partisan. In addition, the views of laymen find effective expression in such periodicals as *Commonweal, Jubilee,* and *Work.*

Cardinal Gibbons, whose great genius lay in correctly assessing the position of the immigrant Catholic and urging him to integrate into American life without losing his faith, was well rewarded. By the time of his death Catholics were generally accepted. With the immigration period ending in the twenties, with Catholics removed from immigrant status by three or four generations, and with higher education among Catholics becoming increasingly common, a change in lay status was inevitable. The next step was to enter the stream of American life and enrich it with the witnessing of Catholic values.

The ferment of the thirties

The thirties were ushered in with restrictive immigration laws and a major depression. The agonizing pains of adjustment to a new land had subsided while the pangs of hunger were creating social unrest. The juxtaposition of these two facts prepared a social climate favorable to Catholic social movements. The Church was no longer insecure about its right to existence. It had sufficient maturity to face up to the problems of the day.

The spiritual basis for action was provided by the liturgical movement, launched almost single-handed by the Benedictine monk, Father Virgil Michel. In 1925 daily missals were rare, as were sermons on the Mass, not to mention community participation. There were no liturgical publications or organized discussions of the liturgy. Before Father Michel's premature death in 1939 these things were realities and a liturgically-orientated piety was becoming a possibility for all American Catholics rather than the preserve of an elite.

The intellectual basis for action was provided by the social teachings of Monsignor John A. Ryan, who provided a philosophical and theological basis for evaluating the social currents of the day. The chair of moral theology at Catholic University and the directorship of the Social Action Department of the NCWC provided platforms from which he reached bishops, priests, and seminarians with his message on social justice, the living wage, and other elements of a just society. A prophet to some, a socialist in clerical garb to others, Monsignor Ryan prepared the way for social movements which would attempt to apply moral principles to the problems of the social and economic order.

With the broad doctrinal synthesis worked out by Pope Leo XIII, and vital spiritual and intellectual bases for action, only a spark was needed to ignite a lay apostolic social movement. This spark came in the thirties from the misery spots of an economically depressed America—it came from the Catholic Worker Houses of Hospitality, the Friendship Houses, and their counterparts across the country.

This was a lay, storefront Christianity which gave flesh, blood, and local color to the Sermon on the Mount. It was Christianity in the raw without the shadow of compromise. The workers literally lived with the poorest of the poor, earning for themselves St. Paul's title to glory: "the refuse of this world, the offscouring of all." Every man in the soup line became Christ, in a prelude of the Judgment scene, "I was hungry . . . I was thirsty . . . I was naked . . . I was a stranger . . ." The staff came to alleviate economic misery or mitigate the evils of segregation and in the process they deepened their life in Christ.

The storefront gave a new dimension to Christianity. It sufficiently awakened and stirred to action a handful of priests and lay people who realized that soup kitchens were not enough to stem the depression or bring about a just social order. With this new insight into Christianity and with the times propitious for the move, they set out to implement the teachings of Monsignor John A. Ryan.

The aim was to go to the root of the problem so that the economic order might become a mirror of social justice. Parish labor schools, city and diocesan-wide institutes and the Association of Catholic Trade Unionists came into being. What was involved was to a wide extent an educational effort, at least

in its first stages. Serious attempts were made to apply the principles of a good social order, as elaborated in the papal encyclicals, to the present scene. When translated into action, this
meant that Catholic laymen were helping to organize the un-
organized, becoming more effective in labor affairs, and flushing
out the Communists from positions of power inside the unions.
Systematic spiritual motivation was seldom given, but through
the work itself dedicated lay people with an apostolic viewpoint
and an enlightened social conscience were produced.

The storefront and social action movements prepared people
for more disciplined and specialized forms of Catholic Action.
The third effort of this era was hardly more than an experiment
before World War II. It was an attempt to transplant the Jocist
type of Catholic Action, so forcefully championed by Pius XI,
to American soil. Unlike the problem-centered storefront and
the education-orientated social action apostolates, this approach
was an avowed attempt to form Christians against the background of their total life, which included work, neighborhood,
home, recreation, and religion.

New directions

With the war over the American economy soared to new
peace-time heights. Full employment and increased real wages
meant more people moving into the middle class economic
bracket. This affected particularly the American Catholic, who
was now removed from immigrant status. The upward mobility
of the American urban-centered Church is obvious. The American Catholic, unless a member of an exploited minority group,
is no longer a manual laborer. Increasingly he is taking the
clean-cut appearance of a congenial and respectable suburbanite. If you want a glimpse of the new American Catholic, con-
sult his pastor. He will give you a warm and glowing account

of his generosity with time and money and his overwhelming concern to see that his children get a Catholic education. Typically, though, he is not concerned with the race problem— in fact, he may have come to the suburbs in flight from it. We must not stereotype the new American Catholic as the man in the gray flannel suit, however, for he may be a card-carrying union member, or even a business agent. But if he is, he may be satisfied with his union status; he is not inclined to fight about it or look upon it as an apostolate. He is, in short, a man of the prosperous fifties, not of the depression thirties.

What has happened to the three efforts: storefront Christianity, social action, Jocism? In the wake of the vast social changes that have taken place in the past fifteen years, the apostolate, too, must change or die. Our storefront missions to the poorest and the racially oppressed still exist, but in diminished numbers. No longer do these centers represent a major training ground for a lay apostolic life. The social action movement of the thirties and forties has had many of its objectives realized. In the North, unions are recognized as a part of industrial life. Added to this, unions have their own education programs for their leaders, and Communism is no longer a major union problem. Here and there Catholic Labor schools have closed their doors.

The third type of apostolic lay movement, however, the one inspired by Jocism, is today a going concern. While the Young Christian Workers were centered in city worker parishes, they made relatively little progress. They found that it is difficult to interest young people in social reform when the shoe does not pinch. However, in the past few years, after much debate, a fresh and realistic approach has been made to young people. The YCW has now accepted the fact that the depression is over and that an apostolate of young adults can and must be built against the background of a prosperous economy and a better-educated community. This has been effected without an abandonment of the social problem, but simply by redefining it.

When the YCW was moving forward only haltingly in the late forties, the same principles and techniques were adapted to family groups and proved highly successful. In view of this success (which will be discussed later, in connection with the family movements), there is no question about the increasing desire of lay people to make an intelligent contribution to the life of the Church. There are many causes, both natural and supernatural, that have contributed to the unique and swift development that has taken place in recent years. Among them one should include the removal of Catholics from immigrant status, increasing years of formal education in Catholic schools, more leisure time, greater economic security, the desire to discuss mutual problems in small groups, the desire for community, the repeated calls of the popes to Catholic Action, the deeper sharing in the liturgical life of the Church, the desire to maintain Catholic family values in a pluralist society, and the need for small groupings in large parishes. All these factors and others have played their part.

The millennium has not been reached. New forms of the lay apostolate will be developed to meet new problems. While it is still extraordinary, one may hear today of a young couple planning to go after marriage to be lay missionaries in South America. While this country is officially only fifty years removed from mission status, its position in world politics is such that it has thrust the American Church into the mission fields. During the past fifty years the American Catholic has heard and responded to countless appeals from the missions for financial assistance. Likewise the American Church has established a distinctive American missionary society for supplying priests and religious for the missions. Now the call is for lay volunteers.

Through the ladies of the Grail, the International Catholic Auxiliaries, and other groups, lay women are screened and trained to give their services to missionary bishops and pastors in tasks for which they are specifically qualified. A new organization, AID (Association for International Development), undertakes to send single men and married couples to the ends of the earth as lay missionaries, bringing the skills of their trades and professions to the under-developed areas of the world. To the teeming lands where formal education is beginning for the masses, it will send teachers; to the new industrialized areas, it will send technicians and trade unionists; to the fledgling democracies emerging from tribal ways, it will send people experienced in government; to the languishing Catholic countries where men think Mass-going unbecoming to their masculinity, they will send couples who will pray and worship together and teach by example the ideal of Catholic family life.

As far as the future of the lay apostolate in the United States is concerned, there is no sign that there will be a reversal of the trend for more and more people to become involved in the mission of the Church as a lay vocation. Indeed, the evidence is very much to the contrary. The shortage of priests and religious will be a constant pressure on bishops and pastors to appeal to the laity for assistance. The layman is acquiring deeper insights into the implications of his occupational life, his neighborhood, his family, as the stuff of a dedicated Christian life and a school of sanctity. Yet large questions face us, involving such points as status for the layman, training, motivation, organizational structure, and lay-clerical relationships. The answer to these questions will in large part determine the future direction and depth of the lay apostolate in this country.

CHAPTER V

Changing Parishes

LAST SUNDAY was Pentecost Sunday. The wind-up of my sermon on the Holy Spirit was an appeal to the congregation to go from Mass intoxicated with the love of God as were the Apostles, who after the descent of the Holy Spirit were accused of being filled with new wine. But what does one do when one is inebriated with God's love? Does he stand on street corners and give impassioned speeches about Jesus being our salvation? These are fair questions which I did not attempt to answer in the sermon. To love God in the concrete circumstances of life requires an analysis of all the aspects of our life. For the most part, we are parishioners, members of families, and pursue some task in the temporal order. In an effort, therefore, to spell out the implication of divine inebriation, we shall pursue our inquiry into these three areas, beginning with the parish.

40

With many Catholics the parish is the seat of sentimental attachment, deep loyalties and rational convictions. It serves as a means of identification. Catholics usually designate the area of the city they live in by the name of the parish there. The parish grade school is associated with memories of devoted sisters patiently leading us through childhood in the ways of the Lord. We may not remember the name of any sister, but our loyalty to the school as an institution touches the inner core of our being. The confessional reminds us of the falls we had and the subsequent good feeling that came as we left the "box" unburdened. The Church is filled with associations that have little to do with the liturgical services. It may be a painting or a window that intrigued our minds. It may be a memory of Aunt Sue's wedding or Grandpa's funeral; the hymn singing, the processions, or an incident when disciplinary action was taken. We may even associate the parish Church with Easter clothes as much as our first Holy Communion or communion with God in our visits to the Church. This is the melange that somehow fuses to form the base for our deepest convictions in life.

As adults, we must take a more mature view of our parish. There is the conceptual view of what an "ideal" parish should be and the sociologist's descriptive picture of what is. We shall begin with the former. To one who understands the doctrine of the Mystical Body, the parish is the localization of Christ in space and time. Through the parish the Christ who walked the streets of Palestine extends and perpetuates Himself in our neighborhoods. To the parishioner, the parish is Christ teaching, Christ ruling, and Christ sharing divine life. The parish is Christ among us.

Since the Fall, first with the Jews and now with the Mystical Body, God has fashioned from the common clay of humanity a People. God's People are not simply the pure of heart, but rather the saints and sinners who through divine predilection have been baptized and adhere to the teachings of the Catholic Church and recognize the Pope as their spiritual father. Collectively, they form a visible community and can be counted and called by name. The parish is a local assembly of the People of God. Christ not only established this People, but He identifies Himself with each segment of it, as well with each member of it. With this People he forms the unity of vine and branches, or of head and members.

The parish exists primarily to give glory to the Father through Christ. The essential work of the parish is the liturgy, which is Christ worshiping and praising the Father through the Eucharist, the sacraments and the prayers of the parish.

Christ is the liturgist *par excellence* and the parishioners are the people for whom He acts at the parish altar. The altar is symbolically Christ and at the altar, in the words of Pius XII, "this close union of The Mystical Body of Jesus Christ with its Head during this mortal life reaches, as it were, a climax."

Community participation in the Eucharist was the earliest bond of Christian unity. It was the Eucharist which brought the Christians together and formed them into an ever-tightening mystical unity. Because the Eucharist is the unifying action of the parish and the Eucharist is the supreme act of Christian worship, the altar is ideally the center of the parish. The mature Christian sees the parish altar as the core and the fulcrum of the parish. Here Christ's priestly prayer, "that they may be one, Father, as we are one, I in them and Thou in me," becomes a reality. In the Pauline sense, the parish is formed at the altar. "Because the bread is one, we though many are one Body." It is the Eucharist that makes and shapes the parish.

At the beginning of our century the white-thatched and saintly Pius X called all Catholics to make the Eucharist the

sun and center of their lives through vital participation in the
Eucharistic banquet, by way of song and by more frequent
partaking of the Bread that makes us one Body. Too long had
the Eucharistic service approximated a cafeteria where everyone
was doing the same thing but apart from each other, not together, as at the family table where all share the same food and
conversation. Since the community aspect of the Mass was so
little understood and since song as a medium of love and a form
of prayer was so far removed from the habits of Catholics, Pius
XI encouraged the recited Mass as an intermediate form. Pius
XII carried forward liturgical reform with unrelenting vigor.
In *Mediator Dei* he gave the liturgical movement its Magna
Carta. He implemented this encyclical with a steady stream of
decrees climaxed with the relaxation of the Eucharistic fast
and the restored Holy Week. The tragedy of the century in this
regard would be for the initiative in restoring the true notion
of the Eucharist to the parish to be left to the popes. This is
a burden for both priest and people.

Second in importance to the altar in the parish church is the
parish's very womb, the baptismal font. From the pouring of
water and the infusion of the Spirit, new life issues in the neophyte and the parish community reaches out to embrace a new
member. The liturgical revival provides a challenge for modern
Church architects to clear away all within the Church, and especially within the sanctuary, which detracts from the altar. But
they must not stop there. The baptismal font, often obscured
in a cluttered sacristy, must be brought to the entrance of the
Church or some prominent place to remind the parishioners as
they move toward the altar that it is from the womb of this font
that they first received the life of Christ, the life that makes possible their participation in Christ's redemptive work in the Mass.
Not only through architecture, but by the living word and the

vivid and public dramatization of these rites must the parish priests proclaim the wonders that God has wrought in forming a People. Laypeople, too, through family observances, are called upon to weave these truths into the fabric of family living.

With Baptism and the Eucharist given their rightful place in the parish church and the scale of family values, the other sacraments fall more easily into focus. Marriage, like Baptism and the Eucharist, must be regarded as a parish affair. Each marriage brings a new unit into the parish and assures the perpetuation of the Church on earth and new worshippers before the heavenly throne. To the parish community, a marriage cannot be simply a private affair. For this reason it is important that all present at a wedding and not just the bridal party receive Holy Communion.

The Christian concept of death as a departure from the assembly of God on earth to the assembly of the saints in heaven must be constantly kept before the parish community by intelligent and prayerful participation in the Last Anointing and in the burial services that join heaven and earth through earnest prayer. The visit of the Bishop to seal and strengthen the neophytes in the faith through Confirmation must be proclaimed in terms of the lay apostolate.

The parish is not only a community of worshipers gathered at the altar, it is likewise a community of believers. Our worship is based on and buttressed by what we believe. It is because of the good tidings which Christ proclaimed that we worship. The parish proclaims Christ, who said "I am the truth." In the formula of St. Augustine, "Christ preaches Christ." The word of God is proclaimed as part of the Eucharistic service in the scripture readings and the Sunday sermons. In 1884, the Third Baltimore Council faced up to the fact that a Sunday sermon was not in itself sufficient for our times and legislated for a Catholic school system that is unique in the history of the Catholic Church. The convent of sisters beside the parish school has been long recognized as the bulwark and tower of strength of the Church in America.

The parish, through the parish school, proclaims Christ to its youth. With a Catholic school for every child as the goal toward which the diocese and parish was striving, the Catholic child in a public school became a step-child. Now, with the proportion of Catholic children in public schools increasing because of the population burst and the shortage of teaching sisters, we must re-examine the status of the child in the public school and make more than a token effort to bring him into the full life of the parish and to give him an adequate religious training course. The Confraternity of Christian Doctrine must be vitalized if Christ is to be all in all. This is a responsibility of the pastor which he must share with the laity, if the job is to be done.

The parish's mission to teach all parishioners through every stage of life needs to be re-evaluated. Among adults the bowling league, the bridge club, and TV have successfully competed with the traditional parish missions and evening devotional services and sermons. It might be closer to the truth to say that the people have not lost their faith, but that the traditional conductors of the faith are losing their effectiveness. It is change or suffer extinction.

Two points are obvious. First, the priests themselves cannot do all the teaching. The laity are called upon to think creatively with their pastor to cut through the log-jam; they must be increasingly willing to assume new duties such as filling the role of religious teachers to our youths. Second, there must be an adult education program, but the teaching of adults cannot be conceived as a didactic encounter with the traditional props of the roll call and blue books. A catechism refresher course would be of little interest to adults who want to relate their faith to the problems of life. Father Joseph Gremillion, a former pastor in Shreveport, Louisiana, developed something called the "Collegium" with a committee of laymen. This is a forum for adults who wish to participate in a discussion of modern problems that have theological implications. One of the first topics was "Genesis and Modern Science," led by the chairman of the biology department of a nearby Catholic university.

Creeds lead to deeds. Truth cannot be imprisoned. Parishioners want to share the truths of their faith with those who will listen. Through crusades like "Operation Doorbell," parishioners ring doorbells like precinct captains, introduce themselves as representatives of the Catholic Church and extend an invitation to visit the parish church on a particular day and hear an explanation of the Church.

The parish witnesses the truth most effectively when its members live by the Gospel. The Catholic family that emphatically takes a stand on the rights of Negroes to live in the Catholics' all-white neighborhood are teaching the neighborhood by displaying publicly their fraternal charity, which is the badge of fellowship in the Church.

The parish must be a community of loving service. If the parish is to witness Christ, it must serve the poor whether they reside in penthouses or flop houses, trailer camps or "Rolling Greens." Through its counseling services and nursing arts it must bind the wounds of those afflicted with mental or physical maladies. It must extend a personal invitation to the lax and strayed to come back to active membership. These are parish services that can be equally dispensed by priest and people, but because of the numerical shortage of the former, it becomes chiefly a lay task. Societies like the St. Vincent de Paul and the

Legion of Mary have been systematically and unpretentiously
providing some of these services to parishioners. Both priests
and people are often tempted to delegate to this hard core of
dedicated people the responsibility for services that can only
be dispensed by those who live among or know personally the
needy.

Since Christ said, "I am the way," the parish must be a way
of life for parishioners. A Christian code of living must issue
from the Christ-life received in Baptism and nourished at the
altar-table. Membership in the Church gives an orientation to
all of life. It brings people together not simply to worship, but
to deepen their associations through education and welfare service. One of the implications of St. Paul's summary of the Mystical Body in the "one Bread, one Body" formula is that our ties
through Baptism and the Eucharist in "the household of the
faith" must be cemented by a network of social relations. In a
pluralist society a minority group, to survive, needs a system of
communication and sharing that expresses group beliefs and
practices.

Underlying the community worship of a parish and guarantee-
ing the preservation of its beliefs and code of living, there must
be a human community. This community is not achieved
through a single contact with the parish community one hour
a week. The community must be achieved through multiple
parish relationships. If the parish has its doors open only on
Sunday it will be a shell, a monument to what could have been
a living community of saints.

Parishes differ

The parish is a sociological reality as well as a segment of
the Mystical Body. It involves parish buildings, a financial structure, and many people playing diverse social roles. It includes

homes, stores, schools, factories, police and fire stations, and playgrounds. It is serviced by newspapers, magazines, radio, and TV. All relationships, institutions, and services that affect the human life of the parishioner hinder or advance his divine life and add or detract from the offering he brings to the parish altar. The parish community, and particularly the pastor, needs the assistance of the religious sociologist to check the effectiveness of his work. Statistics of religious observance, while only one aspect of the sociology of the parish, offer a good starting place. In fact, Pius XII, in speaking to pastors and Lenten preachers in Rome, in 1955, stressed the point:

> In ascertaining needs, avoid superficiality. Superficiality engenders what might be called the working norm of the guess. Its disastrous results are met in every field, not excluding that of the apostolate. To prevent such consequences, a statistical task is required, done with seriousness, with exacting realism and with calm impartiality. . . . Should a pastor rejoice over such a flowing attendance? Undoubtedly he should and rightly so; however, before feeling entirely satisfied he should estimate with sufficient accuracy the number of those who are obliged to attend and who do not. We know, as a matter of fact, that not infrequently an accurate estimate holds unpleasant surprises for a priest concerned with the fate of souls. . . . Having determined the figures, it is necessary to study their significance in order to understand the cause of certain defections or returns. Merely to discover an evil is not enough for diagnosis, without which one cannot speak of a right prognosis and even less of adequate treatment.

When we think and talk about a parish, we are inhibited by stereotypes. We think of it as an intimate fellowship of faith, with the pastor the father of a flock he calls by name; or as an administrative unit of the Catholic Church that dispenses sacraments, baptismal certificates, school and recreational facilities to its registered members or to people who live within certain territorial limits. A seminarian preparing for a life of parish work might look forward to a career combining sacramental ministration with social work dedicated to dead-end kids—fighting delinquency and crime with a bat-and-ball apostolate. The same seminarian might find himself after ordination in an upper middle-class parish with a low delinquency rate, adequate and well organized recreational programs, and a score of people who want to know more about the liturgy and the Bible as a follow-up to a Catholic college education. Another seminarian who conceives of the priesthood as a purely spiritual apostolate may find himself acting in the capacity of a welfare agent dispensing material services to the poor.

The parish as a sociological entity might therefore be best approached by discussing dominant types. The ideal type of parish, where there is an intimate face-to-face relationship, one of spiritual paternity between pastor and people, remains in the rural and small town parish. This relationship is casual but reverent and creates strong ties, even though the influence of the city has reached to the farmer's home or the town hall and taken its toll. The young are weaned from the farm and countryside by the neon lights of the big city. Modern communication makes the rural family more mobile; thus friendships can be based on interests rather than propinquity and community solidarity is weakened. In spite of these disabilities, this kind of parish is still the closest approximation of the relationship described by Christ: "I am the Good Shepherd. . . . I know mine and mine know me."

In a diocese where there are rural areas, small towns, and big cities, a priest's first pastorate will usually be in a rural community or a small town, and the appointment might be nearer the tenth year of his priesthood than the twenty-fifth. This means these areas would have a high percentage of young

pastors and situations that would be more under their direct
control than in a large city parish. These elements are favorable
to the thinking out of fresh approaches to new and old problems. In our farm and small town parishes we have had a
number of such worthwhile efforts.

The city parishes can best be described by using Park's
ecological description of the city. A map of a city can be taken
and with the compass point in the downtown area rings or con-
centric circles can be drawn that divide the city into zones.
A parish type corresponds to each of these circles. The inner
circle circumscribes the downtown area with its stores, offices,
hotels, cultural and recreational centers, and light industry. In
these areas, we have the so-called downtown parish. This is the
direct opposite of the rural or small town parish. The pastor
has few ties with the people to whom he ministers. They are
faces at the communion rail, voices in the confessional, working
people seeking counsel, instruction, or literature during their
noon hour. Rarely is he in contact with his parishioners as social
beings or total persons. Here the priest opens the channels of
redemption outside the framework of a human community.
The downtown chapel or church is a necessary adjustment to
an industrial world that has separated work from its traditional
relationship with the home and with the parish church.

The next ring beyond the downtown area is one of blighted
neighborhoods—decayed foreign strongholds of earlier times
interspersed with warehouses and railroad yards. This ring has
a transient and older population. Its crime rate is high and
welfare services carry an overload. Except for ties between a
few old families, community is non-existent; the area is a human
wasteland. For the Catholic parish here, there are two possibilities: It can keep its doors open and provide services for those
who come, or it can attempt the herculean task of attempting to

create a community, with the parish buildings as a center. Holy Trinity parish, at the edge of Detroit's skyscrapers, is a parish which did just this. Father Clement Kern had the vision, the courage, the faith in human nature, and the charity to undertake the cementing of Maltese, Mexicans, Puerto Ricans, Negroes, and any remaining Irish who had not vanished from Cork Town, into a community that works together and prays together. Everything radiates from the parish house, which performs the services the old city hall did for the immigrants and the downtrodden. The services of the parish seem innumerable: a co-op that is a combination salvage group and a three hundred meal-a-day kitchen for poor children, a credit union with assets in six figures, a maternity guild which provides classes for young mothers in domestic science, a medical clinic staffed by volunteer doctors and nurses, an AA group, an adult education school known as Cork Town College, a legal bureau which deals with "cops" and courts, and a number of clubs that represent the various nationalities in the parish. It is true that Father Kern must reach outside the parish for volunteer help, but it is likewise true that there is a healthy amount of self-help. Lives are reclaimed to the degree that people can be brought back to active participation in these parish welfare services. And the welfare work has brought people back to the parish altar who had previously stayed away.

The third zone is of immigrant settlement, from the second wave of immigration, with two-flat homes and apartments in good repair despite their years. It was not long ago that the parishes here were those with the upper crust Catholics who never had a high per capita income, but were generous people with large families and unmatched loyalty to the parish and deference to priests. The parish loyalty, while breached by parishioners who moved to greener pastures, is still a basis of unity and a rallying point for a pastor who understands the complexity of the social forces that are pulling his parish apart.

In this zone, we often find what is called the changing parish, as compared with the changed parish of zone two. I visited a pastor who had been installed in such a parish only the week before. The neighborhood was in fair physical condition, but in a state of rapid transition from a white to a Negro population. The pastor came there with no elaborate social theories or schemes. He was going to establish community to the degree he could and at every level available. Since all his parishioners are present on Sunday morning, he decided to begin with the Mass. He was going to provide leaflet missals, and also to begin congregational singing of the English hymns provided by the World Library of Sacred Music. He was counting on a core of apostolic white families to arrest the flight of the whites and an inquiry class to interest the newcomers. In many ways, this type of changing parish provides an even greater challenge than the parish in zone two.

The Southern white who has recently migrated to our large industrial centers presents a missionary challenge to the parishes in zones two and three. The newly arrived Southerner has no ties with, or knowledge of, the Catholic Church. He prefers to affiliate with a Holy Roller or pentecostal sect which caters to people in his social conditions. Storefront churches predominate in these areas. Our conservatism and esthetic sense inclines us to reject the storefront mission as too ephemeral. We must remember, nevertheless, that the Church was not wedded to stone and massive architectural forms until the fourth century. The people were considered the living stones of a spiritual edifice. The assembly of God was not a place but a people. Must we demand that the newcomers to our cities from rural areas and with lower educational standards spend a generation or two acquiring middle-class manners, or can we adapt our extra-liturgical services to meet the spiritual and emotional needs of the newly arrived? The possibility of storefront churches and outdoor missions deserve a hearing.

Zone four is the brightly lit area of single-dwelling homes near the city limits. They were established there prior to World War II, but now ranch-style homes appear here and there like new patches on an old garment. There are trees and lawns and occasionally homes with three-car garages. The homes are large, and families of five children or more are not uncommon. The heads of the families are successful in their trade or profession and show great interest in local civic affairs, although at the same time they may show a glaring lack of social conscience when the subject of interracial neighborhoods or aid to foreign countries is discussed. The Catholic parish in this neighborhood has real meaning in the lives of its parishioners. Sunday Mass may draw up to 90 per cent attendance compared with 30 per cent in a zone two parish. The church may be almost filled during the daily Masses of Lent, with reception of Holy Communion by the members of the congregation closer to the rule than the exception. Frequently religious vocations abound.

Beyond the city is the cluster of bedroom suburbs that have flowered since World War II. The suburbs are in zone five, as well as exurbia, which is the residential area beyond the suburbs. There is the mass production suburb that was built for people who could make only a small down payment for a home and who could not afford city rents. It seems too early to predict the future of these low-cost encampments in the land beyond the city. Then there is the Park Forest type of suburb for those in a higher income bracket and with more than a high the way-station at which the young executive's family rests for a school education. This is the social planner's dreamland and

few years in its quest for success. Another type is the old
suburb along the commuter line of the railroad which is now
surrounded by piecemeal developments. The old timers once
eager for new life in the community rue the day they welcomed
the newcomer, who has now taken over their school board,
crowded their schools, jammed their churches, and skyrocketed
their taxes.

The difference between the people of zone four and zone five
is one of age and income. Younger couples have a tendency to
start at the outer rim, and as the years pass on and the family
size declines through marriage of the children, slowly come
back closer to the city. Basically, their aspirations are the same
as in the beginning. They belong to what they consider, in spite
of the disparity in income, the middle class. The differences are
merely in degree.

What seems especially to fascinate the religious sociologist is
the new parish in the suburb. Formerly, the big city parish with
a few thousand families was the dominant parish and had the
greatest prestige attached to its pastorate. Today, the young
curate and the neophyte pastor do not look to the city parish as
the crowning reward which a bishop can confer for a long and
fruitful service. The young pastor is quite content to spend his
entire priesthood in the parish he founded close to or beyond the
city limits. Into those parishes are moving the upper- and middle-income families with youth, some Catholic education, and a
sense of responsibility for the support of the Church. In spite of
the heavy mortgages and small savings this parish is the pastor's
dream. Since it is the dominant type, promising to become more
solidly entrenched and increasingly to give a character to the
Church in the United States, it deserves our attention. Its enor-
mous apostolic potential must be fully exploited.

In the decade of the forties, Holy Cross parish in St. Louis was the goal to which all liturgists eventually made a pilgrimage. With the sociological changes of the fifties, including the new upper middle-class parish, the pilgrims are now making tracks to parishes like St. Richard's in suburban Minneapolis where a Quonset building houses the overflow of visitors. Father Alfred Longley was assigned the task of forming a new parish in a new development in 1952. With no traditions to obstruct his progress, he moved quickly. All Masses are recited or sung. Homilies are the order of the day for parochial Masses. The celebrant faces the people while celebrating Mass. The Divine Office in abbreviated form is recited by representative groups. A book, *God's Family Prays and Sings,* is published by the parish and used by the parishioners for family as well as church use. The complete enumeration of liturgical customs that have been introduced would require much space.

Father Longley's approach to the lay apostolate is through what he calls "little parishes." This effort is probably too new to evaluate, and while not fully developed is remarkably similar to the experiment of a Japanese missionary, Father Joseph Spae, C.I.C.M., who started "Neighborhood Associations" in his new parish in Himejii. A description of this pastoral attempt to form a parish community through a collection of sub-groupings might be valuable to Westerners, who would thus see the universal dimensions of the problem of trying to form a community of hundreds or thousands of families with diverse interests.

In prewar and wartime Japan, the government prescribed the universal establishment of neighborhood associations. Each "tonarigumi" consisted of about ten households which had monthly meetings in the home of a member. These meetings were designed to carry out policies and projects of the government as outlined by the leader. The intimacy of the group became a vehicle for effective action; no one can drag his feet in a small group. In the postwar period, some of the "tonarigumi" have been revived for such civic purposes as festivals, crime prevention, and public hygiene.

Father Spae, noting how well the neighborhood association fits the Japanese temperament, has adapted this form of organization as the basic organizational structure of his new parish. Using a detailed map of the parish and following the natural demographic divisions, he has assigned every parishioner, including catechumens, to a neighborhood association. Monthly meetings are held in homes of members. The group leader is appointed by the pastor and confirmed in office by the bishop. This leader has real status and definite responsibilities. He not only presides over the monthly meeting, he visits each member monthly, keeps the census up to date, visits the sick, plans wakes and funerals, collects monthly church offerings, and in general keeps his finger on the pulse of the neighborhood.

The meetings are carefully planned, first by a small committee of three with the priests, then elaborated by the pastor with the twenty-nine group leaders before the round of neighborhood meetings are held. It is strongly emphasized that this is a strictly parochial organization with no ties to other groups.

The monthly meetings, at which whole families attend, not just couples or young adults, consist of prayers, a hymn, a New Testament reading and discussion, reports on past resolutions, and agreement upon a group task for the month. The project or task is either one suggested by the small committee or one which the group devises. The tasks usually involve the corporal and spiritual works of mercy, with emphasis on providing for the needy and contacting prospective catechumens. Also included in the meeting are the announcements of coming feasts and prayer intentions. The meeting takes an hour, which would mean that with such an agenda there would be little discussion. It is followed by recreation.

With this method, Father Spae has cut through the barrier of bigness and anonymity that destroys the small community and the intimate associations that make life human and meaningful.

Not every pastor is in the enviable position of starting a parish in suburban Minneapolis or Japan. Without an intensive leadership training program and a structure that ties the entire operation together, one might question the effectiveness of "little parishes" in a parish of 1,500 families, a group that in itself would pose a feat of human engineering to organize. Without organic growth the "little parishes" or neighborhood associations would tend to be imposed from the top, thus impeding true lay initiative and responsibility. What is important, and what we are endorsing and underscoring, is the willingness of these pastors to face up to the problem of the impersonal city parish. It is only after such initiative that more perfect models can be made.

Parish Societies

No pastor can successfully weld his parish into a vital assembly of God's people by being the iconoclast who destroys objects of devotion and observances which people have come to regard as necessary for their life in God. The same can be said of parish activities. While we might feel that certain of them are ineffectual in our era, the more prudent approach might be to re-examine them and analyze the possibilities of a re-tooling job.

The parish society might be viewed from the perspective of its program chairman. The task of this person has its peculiar difficulties. There is an hour spot between the business meeting and the refreshments to be filled. The attendance is usually small and the finances for speakers limited, so that big name speakers cannot be attracted. The program chairman is limited oftentimes to the people in the community who are public relations officers for a public service such as the FBI, Civil Defense, or the fire department, to people who have a cause to plead, or to people who are perennials.

The speaker who frequently responds to the pleas of the harassed program chairman gets a good insight into the workings of parish organizations as he waits impatiently for the business meeting to drag to its end. Traditionally, these organizations represent an important part of the parish effort. This could be judged from the importance given to them in the weekly parish bulletin and the pulpit announcements. Generally speaking, the meetings of these organizations are the only official opportunities outside of religious services for parishioners to become acquainted as parishioners, to discuss the implications of their faith in their daily life, and to plan and work together in an endeavor that would promote the objectives of the parish.

Considering the important place held by these societies, the results from them, by almost any standard, are usually disappointing to the priests and laity involved. They are designed to enroll collectively all the members of the parish. From a study of twenty-three urban southern parishes that had an average of 13.2 societies, the results showed an active membership averaging 142 in each parish, or approximately 3.6 per cent of all parishioners who were fourteen years of age or over.

The content of the meeting is further revealing. The work is ground out slowly, with few of the membership outside the officers participating in discussion. Fund-raising, which is certainly one of the responsibilities of lay people in a parish, is often considered the major work of organizations which were founded for another purpose. Fund-raising is a type of participation which most people understand and for which they have competence, but a steady diet of it can debilitate a society. The program chairman seldom has a program in the sense of developing over a period of time a thematic framework for thought and action such as the liturgy, social action, or child guidance. The failure to make use of the techniques of group dynamics and the lack of intellectual content discourage well-educated people from attending. There is little challenge, or opportunity for them to use their unique talents.

After this recitation of the disabilities of our traditional parish societies, the question arises as to whether some should be discontinued and a new type designed to meet the present needs of the parish and its members. Such a discussion should not shock us; Church doctrine is not at stake, only change in the structure of our present organizations. While the body of revealed doctrine cannot change, the organizations can and should change, much as church architecture changes from period to period.

Whether our present societies can be adapted to do the job that must be done for the parish as an institution and the parishioner as an individual, or whether new forms must be introduced, we can distinguish six positive characteristics that should mark a well-ordered parish society:

1. There should be some intellectual content to meetings.

2. The meetings should systematically deepen the spiritual life of the membership.

3. The intellectual content and the spirituality should be related to the actual lives of the members.

4. The purpose of the group should be clearly defined and understood by all.

5. The meetings should be run in such a way that the best techniques of group dynamics are used to afford maximum participation to members.

6. Since the life of a group is sustained by action, the action or service must reflect the purpose of the group and meet a real need of the parish and parishioners.

These criteria seem to have validity for teen-agers and parents, for occupational and liturgical groups. Since complete change of structure cannot be expected to come with one stroke, the gradual method may be the most effective and, possibly, the only way of bringing about long-range changes.

In this matter of reorganizing parish societies, city-wide or supra-diocesan groups should not be looked upon as rivals. Indeed, it may be people who have been associated with supra-parochial organizations who will be best suited to help make the necessary changes. There are many examples of people joining an organization on a city-wide level, and with the experience gained from it later forming parish units of the same organizations. The wide contacts, the spiritual formation, and motivation these wider movements offer should prove a valuable training ground for the future parish leader.

The situation is by no means a hopeless one. It requires rethinking on the part of the clergy and laity. The practical steps that can be taken today and tomorrow depend on the actual situation in one's own parish. The Holy Spirit can be counted on to guide us on the theoretical level and in the field of human relations.

Since a parish is a part of a neighborhood community, it is

expected to make its contributions to that community. The parish itself must establish good public relations with all segments of the neighborhood community from police captain and public school principal to the local ministers and rabbi. Since the common problems of delinquency, youth centers, recreation facilities, relief work, race relations, and housing redevelopment projects are not credal matters, they offer splendid opportunities to clerical as well as lay members of the parish to associate with people of other religions in a relaxed and purposeful encounter with a common problem.

The parish as an entity, not simply individual parishioners, should commit itself to genuine non-sectarian community endeavors. An example of this is the affiliation of the parent-teacher group in the parish with the national PTA movement on both the city and state level. This should not be conceived as window dressing or simply as an effort to create goodwill, but as an unselfish spending of oneself to solve the human problems of the local community. Individual parishioners who have competency should be willing to serve on the many voluntary local civic committees and boards, such as the school committee, the library board, the Community Chest, and the Red Cross.

Young priests and lay people who have been bitten by an apostolic bug become impatient with the modern parish. It has not changed or adapted itself with sufficient speed to meet the needs that are so devastatingly clear to them. They view the traditional parish as the barnacled ship futilely burning itself out in a hopeless effort to pick up speed. In their impatient zeal they are inclined to blunder and then cynically withdraw from the encounter. The parish is slow to change because of the conservativeness that is rightfully the heritage of a twenty-centuries old institution to which Christ committed Himself and His doctrine to be conserved and kept intact.

A parish bulletin tells much about a parish. It gives clues to little changes, seemingly insignificant, such as a list of newcomers in the parish; it is these very minor changes on a wide scale which indicate that the American parish is responding more quickly than we realize to the changes in our space-age society.

Young priests who are anxious for change become pastors. The pastors who are conducting the pastoral experiments today were the impatient young priests of a decade or more ago. They were the young assistants who were reading *avant garde* literature, meeting often with fellow priests and laity to discuss mutual interests, making the slight changes within their scope as assistants, attending conventions or study weeks where frustrated curates could bewail the state of the parish and the longevity of old-school pastors.

This process is still going on. What has changed is the numbers. At a convention in the forties where there might have been a few dozen priests, today there might be two hundred. In another decade these curates who are learning their pastoral theology from fellow priests and lay parishioners rather than from musty tomes will be pastors, too. At the rectory dining room table over which they will preside the subject of change will not meet the arched eyebrows, the set chin, and stoic silence which greeted it when they were curates. In moments of despair, when we think of the rectory door as the entrance to a sealed vault that locks precious treasures from the laity, we must remember that in those rectories reside American-born priests. In spite of the fact that the seminary and a clerical tradition keep a brake on change, priests, too, like other Americans, are adaptable to change.

CHAPTER VI

The Fragmented Family

I WAS ON THE RUE SAINT GEORGE in Paris looking for the office of the International Union of Family Organizations. I found it, finally, in a remarkable office building entirely dedicated to organizations which in some way represent or service the family. Anxious to learn from my hosts about France's bureaucratic interest in the family, I was caught off guard by their desire to talk about the family situation in America. They were fascinated by the research on the family stemming from American universities and by such organizations as the Christian Family Movement. One need not leave his own community, of course, to become aware of the sudden and unprecedented concern for the family. My own city has a number of counselling agencies, both public and church-sponsored, whose main job is to deal with the emotional problems resulting from married life and family relationships.

Every parish priest knows that something has happened to the family. He has had the frequent experience of being called to the rectory parlor or a parishioner's home to meet one or both parties of a shattered marriage which began with the promise of never-ending bliss. So grave has the problem become that large parishes may some day employ lay counsellors to assist the priests in marriage work. The increasing demand for counselling services by married people points to a deep-rooted illness that must be analyzed in terms of change in the family as an institution and of change in the other institutions which affect the family. This analysis is necessary if we are to discover the root changes that have made counselling so necessary.

A study of changes in family patterns brought about by the move of the family from the farm to the city offers insights into our problem. We have always had families living in cities but this is the first time in our history that the majority of people dwell in cities. One of the first effects of the city on the family is to diminish its size. Children put the family at an economic disadvantage. Since the teenager can be of little help to the city family, he loses his economic importance, with the result that the consequent loss of function creates voids which contribute to our high rate of delinquency.

One of the most far reaching changes in the modern urban family is the family's loss of function as a self-sustaining economic enterprise. In other cultures, the family was the producer, distributor and consumer in economic life. A man married not just to have a companion and a mother for his children but to have a partner in a lifelong work operation. The couple married, not simply to be together, but to carry on jointly an economic enterprise.

Daily toil has long since ceased to be a source of unity. Modern industry does not bargain with the family as a unit but with the members as individuals. The family is an unnecessary appendage with which it must reckon. The corporation not only bargains separately for this labor but it removes the work from the home. This centers the day for the head of the household and, to an increasing degree, for his wife, who is the heart of the home, at a place removed from the family's immediate vicinity. Such traditional domestic functions as breadmaking and dressmaking, which give status to a woman as a homemaker, have long since lost this value, thus encouraging wives to leave the home in a search for some activity that the community will esteem.

Not only does modern industry separate husband and wife during the working hours of the day, it separates family from family within the larger kinship circle. The large corporation, like the religious order, sends its "letter of obedience" to its young, newly married employee, assigning him to a distant city and providing a moving van to ease the burden. The moving van is a symbol for the mobility that severs ties between grandparents, parents and children. Relatives can no longer be depended upon for their stabilizing influence on a young family amidst its never-ending series of minor crises. Greeting cards and occasional reunions are too often the only fragile ties that remain.

In a desire for independence, young married couples often break the bonds that unite them to the families of their parents, and their families reciprocate by "not interfering." Out of this mobile and independent family has come the paid babysitter. Families on the move, whether cross country or up or down the social ladder, have little room for grandparents in their declining years. The increase of homes for the aged where people may spend their last years in reasonable material comfort further accentuates the atomization and segregation of the members of the former clan.

The family as a complete economic unit was a school of apprenticeship for its younger members. Mother taught her daughters the domestic arts and father guided his sons in learning the multiple skills needed for a less industrialized era. The new community high schools, which are equipped with domestic science laboratories where girls learn to cook and boys, too, if they so choose, replace what were considered vital functions of the home. Since there is little likelihood that the son will follow the father's trade, our family system has no need to provide for its own apprenticeships.

It is not new in history for women to work outside the home; the great change is in our attitude toward this activity. What was previously considered an exception or an emergency is now a socially approved aspect of American family life. "In 1890 . . . 4 per cent of the country's married women were working; in 1940 there were only 15 per cent, but by April of 1956, 30 per cent of our married women held jobs . . . By 1955, working wives outnumbered the bachelor girls more than two to one." Today there are more than 2.5 million mothers with children under six working outside of the home and about four million mothers with children under seventeen in the labor force of the United States. Economic necessity is the common reason given for the wife's employment outside the home. The concept is an extremely relative one in an era when the ad man teases us with new color combinations and small down-payments. It is the two-income family, as well as those in the high one-income bracket, that is setting the dizzy social pace for the middle-income family. The one-income family finds itself at a disadvantage when its children remind the parents of the spending allowance, clothes, and the gadgets of their playmates who come from two-income families.

One might seriously question economic necessity as the sole, simple reason for married women working outside the home. A discerning wife writes: "If someone pays you in America, that means you're needed. Money has become a symbol showing we are necessary. . . . A wife needs to work to recapture the feeling that she's desirable." This is another way of saying that the household arts have lost their prestige value. This can often be detected in the voice of a woman who confesses that her vocation is "just a housewife."

Earlier marriages, the median age of the wife being 20.3 years, means a longer fertility span but does not necessarily mean a larger family. With the contraceptive device, pregnancies can be "bunched" in the early years of married life so the wife can re-enter the labor force without future interruptions. The median age for women bearing their last child is twenty-six, six years younger than a half century ago. Beginning with age thirty-five, when a mother's youngest child has usually been handed over to the school, the number of women in the labor force begins to rise sharply.

Family life is one of the areas where Catholics feel the conflict between their beliefs and those of the society they live in most sharply. Catholics date and marry at the age other Americans do, but are not "protected" against fertility as easily as their Protestant neighbors. With community support lacking for their Catholic values, compromise comes as easily as falling off a log.

In America in recent decades, modern capitalism has become exceedingly benign and increasingly responsible through its pension plans and welfare programs. Whether union- or company-inspired, these programs have given economic security to a

large segment of the American people. Because of the unpre-
dictability of the business cycle, however, and the inability of
our economic system to provide this security for everyone, the
State has had to move in as the protector and guarantor of human rights. The modern State in the Western world finds itself
taking over what families and local voluntary community organizations did previously. Social security, unemployment com-
pensation, and an array of alphabetical organizations smooth
the rough edges of our economic system. Other countries offer
public health insurance and family allowances for each child.

These gains give men some degree of material security, and
those liberals who fought for them are to be commended for
their concern with the plight of the family. Still, these benefits
can never be viewed as anything more than weak substitutes for
more natural relationships. Every voluntary relationship within
the family system or the larger community that is severed and
replaced by a State service represents a psychic loss. Loneliness,
lack of initiative and function, and the consequent devaluation
of man's most intimate associations, result from cutting off these
meaningful relations and the exchange of services they entail.
Lack of function gives the feeling of lack of self-importance and
lack of value as a person.

The social reformer can claim that these losses to society had
already been suffered before the State assumed its paternal role.
Whether the State severed these ties or whether it was only rem-
edying and ameliorating the damaging effects of an impersonal
economic system which was not geared to strengthening the
family system is beside the point. The reality is that our needs, to
an overwhelming degree, are provided by agencies rather than
through the ties of reciprocal and intimate human relationships.
This represents severe damage to the family, since it no longer

contains within itself the multiple relationships and mutual dependence upon which love thrives.

A Jew in a Nazi concentration camp related his agonizing hardships. The last seventeen days he went without food and the last eleven without water. I asked him how he was able to survive. He replied that it is necessary to have someone to live for. He spent his days caring for a young man weaker than himself. On liberation day he walked six miles to the city dragging the young man, who was unable to walk, after him. "It is not by bread alone that man lives," but by filling the needs of his brethren. It is by performing services out of love that one develops his personality. When the individual cannot or refuses to perform neighborly services, he suffers the loneliness of a person trapped in the pursuit of consumer activities. He has failed to learn the art of loving, which is creative and requires a giving rather than a receiving or a consuming. He has not learned the difference between loving and the desire to be loved.

There is no doubt that industrial life has determined many of the characteristics of the American family and that the modern State has gradually taken over many of the functions previously considered as belonging to the family. Added to these external disabilities is the failure of our law to support the family. When the Protestant reformers rejected the sacramental character of marriage, they opened the courtroom doors for marriage litigation. If marriage was no more than a civil contract, why could it not be dissolved like any other contract, if one of the parties could show sufficient cause? When this loose contractual arrangement is combined with woman's financial independence because of her value to the national economy, we can expect that each year the courts will dissolve hundreds of thousands of marriages and leave the human wreckage to the juvenile courts and the distraught teacher. It is utterly unrealistic to think that because divorce is not permitted by the Church, Catholics will not be affected by it. In 1952, in a survey taken by the *Catholic Digest* among those who showed a preference for the Catholic Church, 49 per cent rejected the Church's teaching on divorce and the use of contraceptives. The values or beliefs of the dominant group will take their toll upon the unprotected minority.

A comparative study of the Jewish ritual and the Catholic liturgy reveals the importance of the home in the Jewish celebration of feasts. The elaborate preparation of ceremonial meals for feasts ties religious belief to the core of family life. The Western gentile world is inclined to look upon the church and the parochial school, rather than the home, as the center and source of religious training. The current religious revival reflects itself in a greater church attendance, but it is highly questionable whether family prayer and family religious customs are to an equal degree being built into American family life. Religious customs tend to be foreign to the home. When this is the case, religion is transmitted without the emotional support of the family unit; it takes on the dead weight of duty and routine and robs the family of another source of unity.

The Catholic Church has always frowned upon mixed marriages. In discussing the matter we are inclined to deal with statistics and arguments from reason. These are legitimate and necessary approaches since they are references to which people respond. However, the greatest argument advanced against a Catholic entering a mixed marriage is that the two will indeed be one in flesh but not one in Christ. The fact that marriage is the image of the union of Christ and His Church means little to most Catholics, because the Church as the Body of Christ is not a compelling force with them. The Catholic marriage as a depository of divine life carries little importance in a secularized world. Because of the break-up of the national parish, wider contact among young people, and less parental control in the selection of mates, we can expect an increase in the number of mixed marriages, with further weakening of the sacramental view of marriage and precious little religious training in the home.

Another vantage point from which to study change in the family is given by analysis of family roles, particularly the roles of husband and wife. Where we have role confusion, we have chaos. In other eras, the husband was the lawmaker, judge, and administrator within his family and the builder of empires without. The mother was the obedient, loving homemaker who rocked the cradle of the child who was to rule the world. For centuries in the Western world there was no question about where authority resided. With democracy, world affairs demanded woman's participation in social and political activities, so that mother must now balance her household duties with her extra-familial obligations. With a measure of financial independence, and the self-confidence and competence which attend it, the wife has subtly, and rightly, commanded greater influence in decisions. In the area of social mobility, and corresponding with her husband's quest for prestige in the business world, the wife has become the social pacesetter; she encourages her husband, often to the point of ulcers, to achieve the symbols of success. The increased importance of his paycheck for the social climb, and his decreased influence in the immediate concerns of the family, helps erase the guilt feeling he experiences through long absences from home because of work or play. This overcompensation for his loss of authority and status within the family results in a further abdication of parental prerogatives so that he becomes a breadwinner and nothing else. Jiggs and Dagwood are caricatures of living realities.

The modern democratic rule of the household runs counter to

the Pauline exhortation read at the nuptial Mass: "Let wives be subject to their husbands." This confusion of roles can only result in family anarchy with Junior enjoying equal status through default of his elders.

This does not mean that roles are inflexible. Husband and wife can preserve their essential roles while making within this limited framework the adaptations which our changing society demands. For example, husbands can preserve their authority and at the same time bring their partners into a fruitful dialogue before every decision of consequence is made. Because women have so many new demands outside the home, husbands need not experience a guilt feeling or a loss of status in helping with the housework, changing diapers, or preparing formula.

To summarize, the fate of the family is no longer rooted in its mastery over the earth, but in an unpredictable business cycle and the mercy of its giant, impersonal protectors. The family then, in spite of all its stainless steel appliances and fringe benefits, is the pawn of an economic system and a benign government rather than the reverse—where the family is the master and the economic and political orders are the servants.

Family stability in other cultures has been created out of many ties. Besides the family as a self-sufficient economic unit, there was custom, which bound people together until death in a monogamous marriage. Today our laws reflect the majority view that a maximum of freedom should be allowed to dissatisfied couples. This permissiveness toward divorce has a fragmenting effect upon the family.

The patriarchal system that bound families of a clan into a single family and accepted complete responsibility for all the lesser units has yielded to the conjugal, small-family system that needs outside agencies to supplement its limited emotional and material resources. The present-day family is based on affection and common interests. This is both its strength and weakness. Affectional love demands a continual sharing and constant communication through many types of endeavors. As a sufficient base for a lifelong union, romantic love, or the physical attraction of married love, has been oversold in our sensate culture.

The modern affectional marriage, which does not have a diversity of supports, puts tremendous demands on the emotional life of the partners. If their love is not genuine and sustained, anxiety and neurosis can result. On the other hand, since their union is based solely on love, it has the possibilities for the happiest type of marriage. But because of the fragility of its base, and the loss of function and fragmentation of the family, the present type of marriage manifests an increasing need for skilled marriage counsellors. But counselling is not enough.

Putting the family together

The Organization Man, and the Organization Family, were first described by William J. Whyte, Jr. in a series of articles in *Fortune* magazine, that became the paperback best seller, *The Organization Man*. The Organization is the giant corporation that moves its employees' families like checkers to whatever spot seems advantageous for company training and promotion programs. The big company is merely accentuating the process of mobility which was introduced by the factory system and the breakup of the family as a self-sustaining economic unit. The loyalty of the Organization Family to the company takes precedence over loyalty to a particular neighborhood or clan. The Organization is the obstetrician that severs the cord tying one generation to the other. The number of Organization Families may not seem great in proportion to all families, but the prestige and mobility of this segment of the population makes it a bearer of our standardized American culture.

In a close-knit neighborhood of Organization Families there is a tacit agreement not to offend by buying a power mower, if everyone else is using a hand mower, or a car in a price range above that of the peer group. The decent thing is to "keep down with the Joneses" or move to a section where one can spend one's entire income without seeming conspicuous. The interesting factor to observe is the mutual dependence that unites these people, to the point that they visit each other's homes without knocking, have no secrets, and solve their problems by the inexpensive therapy of talking things over. Conversations uncover likes and dislikes for cigarette brands, stores, cars, teams, and brands of liquor. This much room is allowed to people who are expected to conform. To what are they expected to conform? To what is socially acceptable to the group, to what does not offend. This can be learned by the verbal symbols picked up from the conversation of the peer group. The critics of this new way of life praise the neighborliness but deplore the sterile conformity which robs a man of his precious individuality. Because the Organization Family is a dominant one and a social pacesetter, it offers an admirable vantage point from which to view the fragmented family.

A psychologist friend argued that the mobility of these people was not an unstabilizing element in their lives, that this type has an adaptive personality. With regard to Church membership we find that these people affiliate with their parish as soon as they arrive at a new location. People who leave a less mobile society, such as a traditional rural society, and enter a fast-moving urban community can be completely uprooted and lose all their moral and religious moorings. My psychologist friend believes, however, that this mobile type has no values to lose but the value of adjustment. To this type changing neighborhoods is like changing coats—no internal transformation is necessary. Yet an easy toleration of conflicting values can result in loss of tension and a negation of all values. This indictment is obviously too severe, but does suggest that conformity can be destructive of personality.

The desire to conform and get along is basically an urge to belong. The fragmented family bereft of relatives, its members away at school and at work during the day, and thus occupied with interests they are unable to share in common, suffers an appalling isolation. It leaves the members with a void that must be filled with something more than a continuous diet of late TV shows.

We cannot restore the family to pre-Industrial Revolution days any easier than we can unscramble an egg. Since the extended family is as extinct as the Neanderthal Man, we must think in terms of the types of alliances that the conjugal family can make. We cannot bring back the national ghettos or establish reservations for the scattered clans of the Murphys, Guggenheimers or Olszewskis. Bridge tables may be still segregated according to race, and even, less conspicuously, along national lines, but a deck of cards is not a sufficient bond to build a lasting relationship among families. To be satisfying, it must be built on abiding values.

The human person is born to love and express that love in both deeds and creeds. There must be a love that transcends the self, the family, and the wider but intimate associations of neighbors, fellow workers, and friends. To be genuine, this transcendent love, which can only be a reflection of the God of love, must express itself in community living or sharing.

With the fragmentation of the family has come a religious revival. Since World War II, church membership has increased to phenomenal proportions. Church-going has become the respectable thing to do. A candidate for public office without religious affiliation is in the same category as a candidate with two wives: he may win but he starts with a serious handicap. The religious sociologist is inclined to take a somewhat dim view of the revival, if by "revival" he understands a humble, soul-searching, mystical experience in which the soul has made contact with the awfulness of the living God. Will Herberg, a sociologist of religion, sees in the current revival a new means of achieving identification. Since nationality is becoming less necessary as a protective agency, people proudly identify themselves on the basis of a particular religious creed.

The fragmented Organization Family needs a transcendent love more than it needs a new form of identification, but there need be no contradiction between the two. If this transcendent love can be found in the framework of a religion which expresses itself in corporate worship and genuine service to the human community, we have a starting point, a way out for the individual who is imprisoned by the shackles of conformity. Religion can be a holy tranquilizer for the anxiety of the upward climb, or it can create in its followers the restlessness of the apostle who is consumed with his mission. It can be used as a power for positive, but egotistic, thinking, or as a way to commune with the thrice-holy God. It can give one the righteous feeling that is the result of regarding material success as a sign of godliness, or it can bring one to his knees as a beggar pleading before the merciful Lord. It can give a warm, cozy glow or lead one into the dark night of the soul.

Christians and Jews can talk about the Judeo-Christian heritage that has kept alive since Abraham the notion of the one true God which both the individual and society need to prevent self-destruction and to reach their fulfillment. But when it comes to dealing with family and education problems, on the day-to-day level where we should share experiences and strive toward a common goal, we find ourselves almost hopelessly divided. While Christians share with Jews the belief in the one true God of Moses, Abraham, and Isaac, and Christian sects share with each other belief in Christ, at least to the extent that they claim Christ as the cornerstone of their religion, in the area of family values there is little possibility that Catholics, Protestants, and Jews can carry on small-group discussions that will result in common actions.

In our day, however, there is a new grouping of families united on the basis of common interests that is becoming the substitute for the extended family and loss of community. Generally speaking, such a group would find itself helpless to cope with an emotion-laden topic such as birth control unless the Protestant members had already accepted the Catholic position.

This new kind of clan must be united along denominational lines if it is to achieve real solidarity, form a sub-culture, and carry out family ideals through common action. Actually, such groups seem to be a demand of our times for Catholic couples. With the protective walls of the ethnic neighborhood crumbling, and with contacts through work, recreation, and civic associations becoming wider and without a denominational base, there must be some form of realignment for Catholics if their family system is to be strengthened and remain intact.

It would be folly to talk about setting up Catholic neighborhood communities that would parallel those of the Mennonites or Amish people. Theoretically, this would preserve the Catholic way of life, but it would also leave out the missionary leaven that has been the ferment of the Church since the first Christians left Jerusalem to set up new communities where the Gospel had not yet been preached. The problem, therefore, is to accept

without misgivings the religious pluralism which is characteristic
of our country, and to enter the stream of American economic,
civic, and leisure activities at the same time as we preserve and
enrich our Catholic ethic.

That many of our Catholic family ideals are out of tune with
the mainstream of American life needs little demonstration.
Obviously, Catholics must be schooled in the Catholic teaching
on sex, marriage, and the family. Catholics have been slow to
come to this conclusion, but today the principle is accepted by
bishops, priests, parents and Catholic educators.

Still, the classroom has its limits. The real teacher must stick
to his last and try to develop the intellect through demonstrating
principles and giving examples of their application. The knowledge imparted and the principles established, however, must be
tested in a completely different atmosphere than that of the
school with its teacher-student relationship.

The girl who in the classroom rejected the idea of a mother
with small children working outside the home must re-evaluate
her position when her former boss asks her back at a higher
salary. In high school she had no idea of what it was to com-
pete with other families for higher standards of living. The situation must be re-examined now. The boy in high school who
accepted the logic of the Catholic view of birth control and at
the age of twenty married a girl whose fertile womb bore three
children in three years is forced to reconsider what he readily
and militantly accepted in high school. He not only receives
subtle barbs from his friends at work and neighbors, but his
fellow Catholics and relatives are prompt to caution him about
taking his religion too seriously. It is plain that education alone
can not sustain the young couple's idealism when the chips are
down. Somehow, Catholic family values must be maintained
and implemented by associations with other Catholics.

CHAPTER VII

Family Movements

Iɴ ᴛʜᴇ ʟᴀsᴛ ᴅᴇᴄᴀᴅᴇ we have coined the expression, "the Ghetto Catholic." This is the Catholic with the partisan, or parochial, view. He votes for Catholics, trades with Catholics, and generally gives uncritical endorsement to anything with a Catholic label. There is reserve or suspicion toward those outside the fold. Historically the ghetto was the segregated Jewish quarter in European cities. Although we think it an infamous practice to force Jews into a ghetto today, it was once a type of segregation that was richly appreciated and prized by the Jews. It provided a social framework which facilitated the observance of religious customs, such as the preparation of food. The close ties of community and religious life protected Jewish values from the ravages of a hostile world. In one city, the Jews annually celebrated the establishment of their ghetto with a special ritual indicating that they recognized it as a privilege.

The ghetto ceased to be a desirable social form when it became transformed from a voluntary to a compulsory institution. The gradual disappearance in Europe during the eighteenth century of the legally protected Jewish ghetto did not take place without some seeing it as a loss. A minority of the Jews doubted that their 4,000 year old heritage could survive among people who would permit them to live where they would.

One of the reasons why the Catholic Church in the United States has the membership it has is that Catholic ghettos were formed. The Catholic immigrants who came to our shores in ever-swelling numbers huddled in large cities where they built their own schools, churches, and fraternal organizations. This concentration of numbers and the freedom of religion which the American Constitution grants made it possible for the immigrants to preserve their Old-World Catholic family values and marry within their own nationality, which meant marrying within their own faith. The Corktowns, the Little Sicilys, and the Bohemias, became immigrant encampments, bulwarks for the preservation of the faith in an alien land.

In the middle of the nineteenth century, Archbishop John Hughes of New York was outspokenly opposed to his immigrant Catholic flock entering the rural colonization movement. It did not take much encouragement to keep the Irish in the big cities, with all the evils of their crowded tenement areas. Theodore Maynard's *The Story of American Catholicism* looks upon this as a colossal miscalculation. He writes: "America today would beyond all doubt have several million more citizens of Irish blood had they only gone to the country instead of to densely populated centers." He refers to it as a "ghastly error which sacrificed ultimate good to immediate convenience." It seems to this writer that the opposite could be argued as effectively. If the Catholic immigrants bought scattered farms through the South and West, the great distances and shortage of priests would have prevented Catholic communities from forming. The Catholic faith best holds together in a social web where people form a solidarity on the basis of deep abiding values.

It is true that 74 per cent of American Catholics are concentrated in the north-east and north-central sections of our country —east of the Mississippi and north of the Ohio—with the greatest concentration in the cities of port entry. These are the areas where we have the most influential Catholic universities and colleges and other institutions of Catholic influence such as the publications of the Catholic Press. These are the centers of Catholic thought which we might not have if we were dispersed evenly throughout the nation.

The cities of this area, with a high percentage of Catholics, may have given us a breed of unscrupulous politicians, but the same cities have also filled our seminaries and convents to the point that surpluses are distributed to other sections of the country. It is highly questionable if the Church in the United States would have its present numerical and institutional strength if its members had headed for the fertile valleys and the plains. For better or worse, we chose the urban ghetto, and it was within this social framework that Catholic family values were transmitted.

As high as we built the walls of our Catholic ghettos, they never became high enough to prevent contact with and influence from the dominant group and the American Protestant ethic. The children and grandchildren of the immigrants had the competitive and acquisitive American spirit of material success built into them. They moved up the ladder, usually, at the rate of a rung every generation, with some jumping two rungs in a single lifetime. This social climb means wider contacts in the educational, business, and recreational spheres of life, and, most important, moving into a neighborhood that has no unifying national or religious character. It means increased mixed marriages, with their debilitating effects on Catholic life.

It would be a mistake to think that, with the rush to the suburbs after World War II, the Catholic ghetto became a thing of the past. In New York, Negroes and Puerto Ricans are forming enclaves in former Irish and Italian strongholds. The national groups which had their immigration peaks in the tens and twenties have left parishes which are still performing vital functions.

Overall, however, the Catholic ghetto of immigrant origin is being replaced by the integrated neighborhood. This challenges the Church to provide a way of maintaining Catholic family values without rejecting the legitimate aspirations of the civic or neighborhood community. Education alone is not the key. Some kind of Catholic family associations seem necessary.

This challenge was put in a practical context for me recently when a newly ordained priest stopped me and pointedly asked me what I thought of the Christian Family Movement. The question was prompted by a couple who had inquired about the possibilities of starting a group in his parish. It was not simply a question of whether it had value in itself and, therefore, was productive of happier families, but what place should it have in a hierarchy of parish duties. He outlined the work to which he was already committed in his parish of 1,500 families. Besides the routine parlor calls, and visits to homes and teaching in the grade school, he had a constant flow of converts to instruct, religion classes for public school children and part-time teaching in a Catholic high school. As he understood the Christian Family Movement he would be working with six couples and devoting to them one precious evening every two weeks. He would be working with what might be called "core families"—what a pastor calls his best families. Would it not be a sinful waste of priestly energy to leave the 1,494 families for the six?

The answer seems simple. Six couples means twelve people. This was exactly the number our Lord chose to indoctrinate for the founding of His Church. On many occasions He left the multitude to spend time alone with this chosen few. The only justification a busy priest can have for spending an evening fortnightly with twelve of his best parishioners is that the operation will be a missionary training course; it will produce family apostles for the parish in the way that our Lord produced apostles for the whole Church. This has been the compelling motive for the Christian Family Movement everywhere.

Social movements such as the CFM are the reactions of a society to some felt and shared need. Catholic family movements have sprung up in different parts of the country since World War II. Whether or not there is a causal connection, the fact is that suburbs, the number and the size of families, and family movements have all increased rapidly at the same time. Even the hierarchy joined in this post-war zest to do something about the family. In 1949, the American hierarchy issued a forthright and positive statement on "The Christian Family." They wrote: "We commend the program of the Catholic Family Life Conference as one means of meeting the evident present need for better and happier homes. Family retreats, Cana conferences, courses on family life in schools and colleges, and study groups concerned with preparation for family life, should be widely encouraged and zealously promoted throughout our country." In practically every diocese of the country the bishop has appointed a priest to promote and coordinate programs to strengthen family life. There is hardly an area in the country where there is not a healthy and thriving family apostolate.

The family program in each diocese has its own history and

emphasis. In Philadelphia, for example, the emphasis is on pre-marital education for the engaged couples, letters to the newly-weds, and parent education. In Washington, D. C., the initial educational effort has become a lay movement. It began with a Cana Conference by Father Edward Dowling, S. J., in 1946. A Cana Conference (the name was coined by Father Dowling) is usually a day of recollection for married couples concluded with the renewal of marriage vows. In these few hours, some of the couples become so fired with the beauty and grace of the sacrament of matrimony that they want others to share this rich spiritual experience. When these couples unite to promote conferences as they did in Washington we have passed from a simple educational endeavor to a family movement.

Through a steering committee and other subsidiary committees, the Washington Cana movement promotes Cana Conferences for married couples, pre-Cana Conferences for engaged couples, and a "follow-up" for couples who have made a Cana Conference. The "follow-up," the Cana Club, is a group of couples who meet monthly in each other's homes and follow a program outline which deals with family topics. The clubs are parish-based and have a chaplain. A parish may have as many Clubs as there are couples and priests who choose to meet.

The Newark archdiocese provides an example of the spontaneity in the beginnings of a family movement. A curate who decided that there was a need for Cana Conferences in his own parish gave the Conferences himself and with parishioners formed a parish Cana Council. The idea caught on quickly in other parishes in grassroots fashion, to the point that the movement was given full status as an archdiocesan organization. The Cana Council includes in its services, besides Cana and pre-Cana Conferences, baby-sitting services, parish Cana newsletters, Cana Mutual Assistance, (a kind of Good Samaritan activity which includes passing on baby carriages and play-pens and the like) Cana family Communion days, days of recollection and retreats for couples, family picnics, dances and Christmas parties. The "Mr. and Mrs. Night" for all the married members of the parish have proved eminently successful in creating parish unity. Well over twenty thousand couples have participated in these programs in the first eight years.

As in Washington, the Cana Conferences in Newark have given birth to another effort designed to continue, deepen, and expand the horizons of the Cana Conferences. The "follow-up" in the Newark Archdiocese is called Cana Family Action. Cana Family Action couples meet monthly in each other's homes and follow an archdiocesan program which is roughly similar to that of the Christian Family Movement in the structure and content of the meetings. The extraordinary efficiency and expansiveness of this movement, which continues to operate with its original freshness, comes from its couples; they still live in wonder and awe of their vocation in the Mystical Body as married people, a concept that was gradually unfolded to them in the early Cana meetings. The Newark family movement represents more than idealism and efficiency. It is a monument to clerical belief in lay responsibility. "Cana doesn't use its lay people just to serve cake and coffee," says one of its spokesman. "Lay men and women are integral to Cana."

Archdioceses like Buffalo, Hartford, New York, Louisville, Milwaukee, San Francisco, Los Angeles, and a host of dioceses, have histories of family movements which began with a few couples and priests who had the courage and the vision to blaze a trail for hundreds of other priests and thousands of other couples who were eager to discover the riches of Christ in their vocation. However, the Archdiocese of Chicago, because of its early start, its strategic geographic location, and the climate that had already been created by Catholic Action groups before a family movement began has taken the lead in the family movement field.

In Chicago, Cana and the Christian Family Movement are twin movements with separate structures but interlocking directorates and a common mailing address; one did not beget the other, as happened in Washington and Newark. The Cana services have expanded to the point that over one-half of the engaged couples of the archdiocese now make a pre-Cana Conference before marriage.

The Christian Family Movement grew out of a men's Catholic Action group which focused on the family because that was the one thing in which the members had a common interest. Soon the wives were brought into the group and the leadership and guidance of the movement became associated with a young attorney and his wife, Mr. and Mrs. Patrick Crowley. From meetings in a Loop law office the movement spread to the parish, with parish priests serving as chaplains. Without the services of a professional staff, the movement spread across the country and then across both oceans; in less than a decade, it became a world movement.

The beginnings in each parish are purposely small and without fanfare. Not until six or eight couples have been meeting in each other's homes for six months to a year are new groups formed. The original members form the new groups and assume responsibility for their continuance. This provides the possibility of many groups in a single parish, with the chaplains attending as many meetings, or parts of meetings, as time allows.

The content of the meeting includes a scripture discussion which usually terminates in some resolution. It is followed by a liturgy discussion—a short doctrinal discussion on the Mystical Body, the Mass, or some related subject. Reports are then made of unfinished business, and urgent community needs are brought up and acted upon. This brings the group to the heart of the matter—the social inquiry.

The social inquiry has three parts. The first, the "Observe," asks a series of questions about a factual situation. If the subject is neighborhood recreation, the members must do some on-the-scene reporting before the meeting, such as talking to parents about facilities and services, interviewing the park board or the local playground director to obtain detailed information about the situation. When the members have compiled and assorted these facts, a realistic picture can be presented to the group.

The inquiry then moves on to the second phase, the "Judge," which is an analysis of the problem in the light of the Gospel and papal teachings. It is here that the priest's contribution is brought to bear. Usually he prepares this part of the meeting in advance with the discussion leader and in the meeting itself adds his comments to the discussion—but not until the end, so that he won't silence the lay people by playing the role of the expert. The "Act," the third and final phase, terminates the inquiry with an action that is directed toward a Christian solution of the problem that was presented in the first part.

Through the social inquiry CFM links life in the world with life in God. Writers and preachers usually discuss this relationship in general terms. They repeat with St. Paul that "the will of God is your sanctification." But what, concretely, is the will of God? How do we determine it? Does a priest tell us how to vote, what job to take, what car to buy, where to live, what stand to take on foreign aid, and whether to be permissive or authoritarian in the raising of children? The "will of God" can be a glib phrase, especially on the tongues of those Christians who through ignorance of its social teachings, work at cross-purposes with the Church.

People are told from the pulpit that they sanctify themselves by living according to their state in life. But what are the specific requirements of this state? Actually, a layman has many different "states" in life. Work, home, social, and community life all make different demands on him. To find the will of God in each of these areas requires sharp analysis. Because of the complexity of modern civilization, we need wide experience and a large number of facts before we can make valid judgments on most matters. A practical judgment about a course of action can only be a here-and-now attempt to define a pattern of Christian action.

Cultural patterns change rapidly in a dynamic culture like ours, so that most of our answers to the problems posed by those patterns are not as important, in the long run, as our method of finding the answers. This method is the social inquiry, which might better be called "role analysis." We investigate each role we play, to find out what the will of God is for us here and now and what apostolic opportunities this situation presents to us.

The inquiry method of Catholic Action stems from Canon Cardijn and the Jocist movement. In the inquiry the real is contrasted with the ideal; there is thesis and antithesis, setting up a tension. In the language of Cardijn, a concrete situation involving a person is contrasted with that person's dignity as a son of God. If the situation is at odds with the Gospel, a contradiction is brought to light. This is the conflict our Lord predicted for His followers.

The inquiry may make non-conformists out of well-adjusted neighbors. For example, through an inquiry on the race problem, people may see that the segregated housing policy of their suburb is in violent conflict with the story of the Good Samaritan. For a housewife to inform her neighbors that she had changed her views on what constitutes an ideal neighborhood, might destroy long-standing friendships in the community.

The social inquiry thrusts people into life. Since the Desert Fathers, there have been Christians who wanted to withdraw from combat in the world in their quest for holiness. Even CFM members sometimes want to use the Gospel and liturgy discussions as protective cloisters by spending the entire meeting on them at the expense of the social inquiry.

Through the social inquiry, however, problems are brought into focus that Catholics often have a vague awareness of, but which they seldom face squarely. As Catholics, after all, we are at a disadvantage in our society since our family values conflict with those of the dominant American family system. Without group support and a medium through which to articulate tensions, Catholic families find themselves making compromises almost unwittingly. Just as in marriage husband and wife support each other, so in the larger community Catholic families support one another by openly taking a position on matters in which the community at large offers no support. Through CFM, Catholic couples find a security that gives them courage to take part in the still larger community, through a disinterested service in every phase of living.

Most people stumble into CFM. They join simply because someone asks them to come to a meeting in someone's house. Without warning they find themselves discussing the Gospel. This proves a novel and thrilling spiritual experience. Christ had been a Person whom they heard about from the pulpit or through the blacked-out slide of a confessional. Now, in CFM, Christ becomes someone familiar, discussed with like-minded people in the congenial and familiar setting of a neighbor's living room.

Under these circumstances, our Lord's words have a truer ring and a more pointed application. He seems to talk through the group about family life. On the basis of the Gospel discussion a gradual overhaul job is done on the group's spiritual life. During the beginning meetings, particularly, resolutions are made and kept with regard to such things as the morning offering and patience with the children. The social inquiries force people to take a second look at their neighbors in the block, to consider the effect of TV on children, and the like. As a result CFMers welcome newcomers, make some needed adjustments in the recreation pattern of the family, maybe set up a sitter service, or give a hand in the campaign to put Christ back into Christmas.

As uplifting and as stimulating as these experiences are during the first few years of CFM, there comes a crisis in the spiritual odyssey of the CFM couple and the chaplain, and even in the parish unit and the diocesan federation of CFM groups. The inquiries seem to cover pretty much the same problems over a period of years. Actions seem to be the same kind, small, unimaginative, and perfunctorily performed. CFM no longer seems to give the spiritual lift it did formerly. The point of diminishing returns has arrived and priests and people seem to be getting less out of the bi-weekly meetings than the effort required to attend them.

A social movement generally goes through three phases. First there is the clear vision of a need to be filled, combined with the sense of mission of pioneers; second, wide organization and acceptance; third, institutionalization and stagnation. Either the vision fades with those who follow in the footsteps of the founders, or with the passing of time the need is no longer acute.

Anyone deeply involved in a movement needs to take time out from the day-to-day operations to view his work from a long-range perspective.

The author had such an experience some time ago when he joined a group of some fifty Christian Family Movement chaplains who were gathered together in a rectory basement to give their movement a critical appraisal. CFM had been in operation on a national scale less than a decade, which is little more than an overnight stop in terms of a social movement.

At this study day, not a word was mentioned about expansion. The group was concerned more with the direction the movement was taking than with the speed at which it was growing. The proof of a movement is not in its numbers, but in the effectiveness with which it does its job. There can be a point of diminishing returns, when any increase can have the effect of adding water to wine. Even Isaias (at least as he is quoted to us by the Church in her liturgy) warns of the heresy of numbers. "Thou hast multiplied the nations and thou hast not increased the joy." CFM's very success was a subject of scrutiny for the group.

What does explain the forest-fire growth of CFM? First, there is the sociologist's explanation with his professional jargon: the tremendous mobility of people in this country resulting in the loss of the extended family or clan; in-laws scattered across the country creating voids in each family unit; upward mobility destroying the national ghettos and stratifying communities on economic lines. The role of the parish, too, has changed. On the whole, with the exception of the parish school and the financial drives that bind new families to new parishes, parish life is pretty much reduced to the dispensing of the sacraments and Sunday Mass.

Because of these voids in the family, work, and parish communities, there is a tremendous urge on the part of families, particularly young families in new housing developments, to find community on some level. At the same time, there are people in these areas with a deep Catholic background, often much Catholic education, who not only want to cling to Catholic ideals but to establish community at this high level. They see the challenge to their faith in the area of family ideals. They want to root this Christian community on a parish basis, but not without some modification in the structure of our "traditional" parish societies.

Our age has been characterized as an age of discussion. American Catholics are generally docile, but they prefer to talk things over rather than be told the answers. Another characteristic of the American people is a natural generosity that expresses itself in services. We not only have drives for cancer, heart disease, TB, polio, muscular dystrophy, with their crops of volunteer workers, but we have in every city an increasing number of service clubs such as the Rotary and Lions. Naturally speaking, if an organization is going to hold people, it must make them doers.

CFM responds to all these needs or urges of our nature, our faith, and our times. It brings couples together on a parish basis, not only to discuss the Gospel and its implication in family and neighborhood life, but it makes them doers of the word. Its adaptability to the American ideals of efficiency, progress, perfectibility, and democracy can be seen in its masterful use of group dynamics. I remember a foreign observer being critical of what he considered CFM's preoccupation with the mechanics of how to run a good meeting. CFM's answer is that if a secular technique can help them communicate, then it can become a vehicle of charity.

If CFM does all these things, one would think that the CFM chaplains who met that day would be applauding each other. Not so. One speaker, a young priest, used words like these: "Is CFM changing the suburbs, or are the suburbanites changing CFM? Is CFM being scaled down to their ideals, or are the ideals of Christ with their revolutionary impact upsetting people so that even if they do not leave home for the Gospel, they give all to follow Christ?"

The young chaplain's words were as challenging as the widely quoted question of Peter Viereck: "Is the honorable adjective 'Roman Catholic' truly merited by America's middle-class-Jansenist Catholicism, Puritanized, Calvinized and dehydrated?"

The middle-class Catholic, with his record for Mass attendance, frequent Communions, generosity and docility to authority, was investigated at our chaplains' meeting. With all his virtue, does this middle-class Catholic have a restless concern for the poor in his own city, for the ill-housed Negro, for the hungry in every corner of the world? Is he not a Puritan in his approach to the poor? Is CFM giving the middle-class Catholic an integral Catholicism that makes him want to spend himself for Christ's wretched everywhere, or is it confirming in him a Calvinistic complacency and righteousness? Tawney's words describing the Puritan movement of the seventeenth century have point today in suburbia.

The chosen seat of the Puritan spirit seemed to be those classes in society which combined economic independence, education and a certain decent pride in their status, revealed at once in a determination to live their own lives, without truckling to earthly superiors, and in a somewhat arrogant contempt for those who, either through weakness of character or through economic helplessness, were less resolute, less vigorous and masterful, than themselves.

Indeed, the priests' study day might have given an observer
the impression that CFM is the preserve of the middle-class
suburbanite. While the movement may have a particular attraction for such people, it belongs to all and is reaching all. I remember a few years ago attending a picnic of a CFM group
from the heart of Chicago's Negro ghetto. Because of their
economic struggle, CFM became a struggle. It is not easy for a
man to attend meetings who has to work at two jobs to support
his family. Joining the Negro CFM group that day were a number of CFM couples from one of Chicago's North Shore suburbs. They were there lending a hand because they wanted
CFM to penetrate the lowest economic and social strata. These
CFM suburbanites were restless in an apostolic way to destroy
the racial ghetto. CFM had given them a bit of the mystic's
vision and the prophet's passion.

The identification of the family apostolate with the suburbs
disturbs many of the people who have given themselves to this
apostolate as unselfishly as any storefront or Skid Row apostle.
They never intended that the family apostolate should be the
preserve of any one stratum of society. Yet a movement that
cuts across social and economic lines must draw upon the best
talent in the Church for its leadership. Generally speaking, the
people most capable of such leadership will have higher education and will occupy responsible and rewarding positions in our
economic society. Residentially, these people tend to be strati-
fied according to their economic status, and for this reason we
must look increasingly to the suburb in the future. Lay saints
can flower in Everdawn Heights as well as on the sidewalks of
New York. In fact, a case might easily be made that Everdawn
Heights should be a better anteroom to heaven than a neighborhood where social conditions have spawned great injustice and
social dislocations.

Still, it would be a disservice to the Church to identify CFM exclusively with the suburbs. Every kind of parish needs apostles of the family. These apostolic families must somehow be created to form the parish leaven. It might take greater effort on the part of the priest and organizing couples to reach people who are less inclined toward discussion-type meetings, but with patience such people can be won over. It might be added that the problem of the lethargy of the inner city is not exclusively a problem for the Church. Our city civic leaders likewise bewail the fact that the suburbs are developing in such a way that there is increasingly less need for the services and cultural advantages of the city.

CFM chaplains are realists. They know that CFM is not a panacea. It is not a substitute for adult education or a course in Christian Doctrine. It is not an interracial council, a local liturgical movement, or a chapter of a social action movement. Nor does it lessen the importance of those apostolates; on the contrary, CFM needs them acutely as resource agencies.

It seems that the genius of CFM lies in its ability to get across the conclusions of the specialized groups to a large number of people who might never have heard of these groups or if they did, might scorn them. CFM works like the precinct committeeman who rings the doorbell and will discuss issues in the living room informally and with a local twist. If the highly specialized apostolates did not exist or if CFM fails to use their services, CFM might be perpetuating what Viereck's question suggests, or be limited to discussion clubs or retrieving lapsed Catholics, thus entering the specialized field of the Confraternity of Christian Doctrine and the Legion of Mary and multiplying movements without necessity, instead of embracing its present wide sweep of all human and supernatural values.

Another danger is a lack of intellectual approach to CFM. Although the movement is not an intellectual apostolate, members must read according to their ability on a wide variety of subjects, if there is to be depth to the movement. While CFM is not meant to turn out scholars, it must avail itself of the scholar's conclusions. It is good to have such top sociologists as the Jesuit Fathers Fitzpatrick, Thomas, and Fichter, making their scholarly contributions to CFM in the way of speeches, articles and books.

In practice, how effective is CFM in a particular parish? The answer I gathered from our study day was that it is as effective as the chaplain is in understanding his priestly role as prophet. The lay people do the recruiting, make the sacrifices to attend, and ultimately perform the services or actions agreed upon. But how the CFM is manifesting the real spirit of the Church, locally, depends on the vision of the chaplain. His part is to help the members discover the mind of Christ, see the mission of the Body of Christ, fire them with the fire Christ cast upon the earth, and create a restlessness in them until all is Christ. Without this exercise of the prophetic role of the priest, CFM is just another parish organization.

CFM plays the role of a creative minority in a parish and in a diocese. CFM itself may not make the necessary changes in the parochial and diocesan institutions, but its members are ceaselessly at work studying the situation, uncovering new facets, suggesting fresh approaches. Gradually those not associated with the group see what must be done and take advantage of the climate the group has created, and the change is made. The hope of the Church throughout history has always been in its creative minorities—initiating, suggesting, always obedient and never interested in personal conquest. The CFM is not only a creative minority but it is also a new and vital type of ghetto wherein there is constant interaction of Catholics as a base for outward action in the wider community. The movement is rich with promise.

CHAPTER VIII

The Teens and Change

These are teen times. Everyone is concerned about this strange new creature. If the man from Mars comes under the gaze of the journalist, I don't think the latter will be more fascinated than he is with his present discovery. Roto sections every week tell us what the teens do on dates, how much they spend, what their preferences are in clothing, hair styles, music.

Civic leaders castigate the teens for falling down and worshipping a rock-'n'-roll idol. The same civic leaders campaign for swimming pools and the frills of modern education that impose a tremendous burden of school bond issues on the small property owner. The civic leader is not at fault as much as the public which votes against such basic civic improvements as a drainage system, or against a decent wage for firemen, while one school referendum after another passes because of a sentimental feeling that "nothing is too good for our kids."

Everybody but the teen seems to be concerned and even alarmed about the teen. Behind it there seems to be a secret envy. Father Time has taken his toll upon our lives. He has stolen from us our youth. Our own teenage years have vanished into thin air like the soap bubbles of our childhood. As the bubbles of our dreamland break, there is a sigh of regret followed by a feeling of righteous indignation. When the teens fail to act as mature adults, we point to the community centers we build for them, the cars we buy for them with our hard-earned money, the sets of encyclopedias we have been persuaded they need. We want to take away their toys in these moments and we might, if it were not so painful to us and them. A teen can be respectful to his elders, as when he refrains from laughing at a graying teacher or a paunchy father who pontificates about how hard he had to work as a youngster, compared with the soft life of this younger generation. The youngster knows the hard life, usually exaggerated in the telling, was a matter of necessity, not choice.

Imitation is the best form of flattery. Notice the clothes styles of young grandmothers. Are they cut to give the appearance of matronly dignity? Or could their dresses be as easily worn by juniors in high school? Why does a woman "slenderize," and put her health in jeopardy? Is it to look like a woman or a high school senior? Grandmother is imitating granddaughter, instead of the reverse.

Some time ago, I attended an athletic banquet in honor of a high school football team with only a mediocre record for the season. An All-American quarterback was the speaker and the two head tables were stacked with big-name people. The grand ballroom of the hotel was not big enough to seat the people who gladly paid five dollars a plate to sit at tables in an overflow lounge adjoining the hall.

The next morning these football heroes sat before me in our sociology class. We tried to make a sociological analysis of what we had taken part in the night before. Frankly, the boys were quite confused as to the meaning of the whole affair. They were teens who played football because they loved it or social pressure compelled them to. In no case did they feel the town should have turned out for them.

I made the suggestion that at the end of our sociology course, when our term papers would be completed, we have a big celebration at the same hotel. Some of the term papers would represent beginning efforts at real scholarship. The boys would have looked up the *Readers' Guide to Periodical Literature* and become acquainted with the card index of the public library. It is true that their work would represent no real research, but it would be a foundation upon which they could build in later life to analyze and solve social problems both intellectually and practically. If such was accomplished through these term papers, would it not be equally fitting to have a sociology banquet for all the students, the parents, and the people interested in social thought, and have the President of Notre Dame University as our guest speaker? I fear the number of people we could get to such an affair could be accommodated in the cloak room of the hotel without disturbing the coat racks.

The discerning reader, I am sure, already grasps the burden of these lines: There is nothing wrong with the teenager that is not essentially the fault of the adult community. When we set aside the teen for castigation, we seem to forget he is what society has made him. He is doing what we have encouraged him to do. We forget that there is no such thing as a lost generation, that is, one separated from another. All generations blend to form a whole. We are all of a piece.

Society is already organized before we become a part of it.

We try to learn as well and quickly as we can what it expects of us, and how we are to do it. We do not enter it with a critical attitude and a whole scale of values with which to judge it; we are gradually ushered into it. Parents want their children to adjust to it; they don't want them to be non-conforming, unadjusted "squares," any more than the children do. In fact, parents can be overly anxious about the problem of adjustment. If Mary does not have a large number of callers, or a "steady," mother can be a worried, harassed woman beating her breast for having failed Mary somewhere. In this case, if it is not the parent who established the social pattern, it is the parent who is strengthening it and perpetuating it.

When rock-'n'-roll was the rage, a first-page newspaper article appeared with the caption, "3,700 Rock-'n'-Rollers Wreck New York Theater." So violent did they become that "175 police were hard put to maintain even the semblance of order." Certainly no parent approves of this behavior. Yet can we completely absolve parents from all responsibility? Some day a team of sociology research experts may do a study of one thousand homes of teens and study the art forms or interests of the parents. What kind of music, if any, are the parents interested in? Do they have an appreciation of what true beauty is, or are they, too, victims of our standardized and sensuous culture? Likewise, those who bewail comic book reading might find a study of the reading habits of the parents of comic book addicts revealing. I think the New York theater demonstration might be better understood in terms of a vacuum in the teenager's home and school life that was unfortunately filled in an explosive and degrading way.

I believe that adult glorification of the teen as a lovable, crazy, mixed-up kid is partly responsible for rebellion and what is popularly called juvenile delinquency. The typical senior prom as an American teenage institution is a form of rebellion, one that is organized and highly approved. Parents and schools try futilely to keep it within reasonable limits, but every senior wants to make his prom a Monaco extravaganza. The teenager will have his way after all we do for him. Probably this is the crux of the whole problem of rebellion. They subtly resent our doing things for them instead of our helping them to develop their own creative powers.

If adult society has such an overriding control in shaping teenage life, the logical place to begin improving that life would be in the home. A great youth leader reportedly said, before his death, that if he had his life to live over again he would devote it to parents rather than teens. How often have I debated issues in social science classes with students, when it was really the parent with whom I was arguing. The son was defending the position of the father and at the same time absorbing the tensions that really existed, not between himself and me, but between the father and myself. It would have been fairer to both father and son if I could have carried on the dialogue with the responsible party.

A valid approach to our youth problems seems to be in a renewed vigor in our family life. As I write this, I can hear the answers I have received from teens. "Home is boring. There is nothing to do there." I suppose the parents might answer. "We have TV, magazines, and everything. We buy them anything they need." This answer brings us back to the conclusions we drew about teenage rebellion. Youngsters want to do things rather than have them done for them. "To be creative" is the phrase. It might mean permitting a boy to have a workshop and old pipes, electrical equipment, or engines in the basement rather than forcing him to play baseball like every other boy.

Conversations with parents can be creative. Father and son,

mother and daughter, should be able to establish common interests. This does not mean the father is to forfeit his parental role and become a brother, or mother become a sister. Companionship can never rule out the firm hand of authority. The communication skills will profit the family little if the parents do not have many and varied interests in life. With these interests and our patient efforts at communication, teens can learn that parents are not relics of a dinosaur era and parents can learn that teens are not the mysterious, unpredictable creation of a new dawn. The generations are closer than we think.

When the steady-goers have broken up, when girls are wearing modest dresses, when rock-'n'-roll records are smashed, horror comics are torn up, and only Class A movies are patronized, the Christian millennium will not have been reached. Purity of thought, word and deed, and modesty of dress are concerned with but one virtue, and not the greatest of them. We can be pure but fail to love God and our neighbor. We can so occupy ourselves in the fight against sex deviation that we can forget the essential reason for our existence. Spiritual development means growth in the virtue of charity.

Parents must teach charity by their example. Bringing foreign students to dinner, defending minority rights, visiting the sick, sending teenagers on errands of mercy, picking up clothes for the poor cannot help but result in a spiritual experience for the high school student. Children respect their parents and thus learn charity from them when they see them engaged in an apostolic group like the Christian Family Movement or some similar work such as the Confraternity of Christian Doctrine, or Cana Clubs.

Young people need apostolic motivation. Parents cannot push their children into organizations such as the Sodality, the Young Christian Students and the like, but they can do much to encourage them to join and to buoy them up when they are not meeting with success. Some form of apostolic activity can be of immense formative influence in teenagers' lives; it can perfect and finish what parents and teachers have begun in earlier years.

It is true that the parents have the major role in establishing the kind of family living we have been advocating, but it is also true that the teen has a bigger stake in the home than he thinks. He must bring his stone every day to the building of this common edifice, to the Christian family of which he is a member. Some day these teens will have the controlling interest in a family venture of their own. It is during high school years that they must prepare.

In a high school marriage course I asked the class why students insisted on going steady when the older generation shakes its head in disapproval. A discerning student answered, "Because we want to be like others. We want security in our dating life. Because our elders tell us not to." Briefly, the answers were: conformity, security and rebellion. Another student said: "But, Father, conformity is taught to us by our parents." "Yes," I added, "and so is security." These are the twin tranquillizers of adult life. This is probably the saddest indictment of our youth. Only rebellion distinguishes them. It provides the only force to move them to something constructive. Conformity and security immobilize youth and turn them into smug, complacent, unimaginative people.

When teenagers start high school, they leave the protective environment of the home, the neighborhood, the parish and the parish school, and embrace a new world. Extracurricular activities, new hang-outs, and wider acquaintanceship tend to keep them from home. This takes place at a time when deep biological changes add special complications in the life of the adolescent boy or girl. The combined changes, social and physical, bring about disorganization. Docility gives way to a questioning attitude towards life. These new attitudes call for a change of strategy on the part of adults.

The guides of youth should bear in mind, first of all, that this rebellious spirit is nothing new. In the year 4000 B.C. an Egyptian priest wrote: "Our earth is degenerate in these late days. There are signs that the world is coming to an end. Children no longer obey their parents. Everybody wants to write a book. The end of the world is near."

3500 years later there does not seem to be any improvement. Socrates (470-399 B.C.) wrote: "The children now love luxury. They have bad manners, they show disrespect to their elders, and love to chatter in places of exercises. They no longer rise when their elders enter the room. They contradict their parents, chatter before company, gobble up dainties at the table, cross their legs, and are tyrants over their teachers." This was nearly 2500 years ago.

Actually there are many observers who think that the present generation of youth are so jaded by having things made easy for them that they no longer show the normal and healthy manifestations of creative rebelliousness. One sociologist is concerned with the "relative lack of revolt among young people against the *cars* of their parents. They seem not to want hot-rods: they don't mind driving their parents' Buick and they wouldn't be unhappy with one of their own."

William H. Whyte, Jr., in *The Organization Man,* expresses concern about the overwhelming number of college graduates who are satisfied to take a job with the organization that gives them womb to tomb protection rather than strike out on their own in a work that may not be as financially rewarding but presents a challenge. Dr. Henry P. Van Dusen, president of Union Theological Seminary, holds that youth suffers from "a

lack of worlds to conquer. Youth cherishes no extravagant ambi-
tions. . . . They are tolerant of almost everything . . . shocked
by nothing."

It is the nature of man to be dissatisfied or to rebel. The world
would destroy itself if it had no rebels, people who want to
change things. Bland young people who are satisfied with everything are ordinarily not the best prospects for Catholic Action
movements. The apostolate creates and feeds upon restlessness.
The rebellion and restlessness must be directed into creative,
apostolic channels. We need young rebels for Christ. He said, "I
have come to cast fire upon the earth. . . ." He predicted that
if his Gospel was lived it would cause division at home. Woe
to the world if it lacks young Christian rebels!

I was at a meeting of high school teachers who sadly la-
mented the demise of the young rebels in our Catholic high
schools. They recalled the late thirties and early forties when
students gave up their Saturday mornings and came miles to the
center of the city to express their dissatisfaction with the world
of their elders. They wanted to find the mind of Christ and of
the Church on current social problems and to complete their
discussions with decisive action. The teachers bewailed the
fifties with their smug complacency. They wanted to know how
they could spark another generation to the white heat of Christ's
love.

We have discussed what parents might do to encourage crea-
tiveness. But, actually, youth must do the creating itself. The
home, the parish and the school can provide an atmosphere or
a permissive attitude. Youth must face up to youth problems
and see in them an apostolate. If we talk about a family apostolate or a priestly apostolate, it is equally valid to talk about a
youth apostolate. While youth did not create the world in
which it lives, it must assume responsibility for the changing of

it to the degree that this is possible. Young people must have their own apostolic movements if the Church is to train people for adult apostolates.

Someone may say that what is needed is a good sermon or series of instructions by a priest who understands youth and talks their language, someone who can speak with authority and persuasiveness about the rights and wrongs of teen goings-on. This solution is too simple. It is true that the priest is the guardian of the moral law. He sets down the general principles. But there is seldom disagreement on principles; the difficulty is in applying them to particular cases. What happens when the circumstances change? Where is the priest to tell us what to do in these new circumstances? The problem is really of another order: People develop not by being told what to do but by doing it.

Nor can the school provide the whole answer. Unquestionably the Catholic classroom prepares people to reason soundly and to have ready answers, but the classroom can never give experience in living; this is not its mission, which is to deal with thought rather than action. The Christian life, however, is not learned; it is lived.

Youth must develop apostolic leadership through contact with other youth. Catholic youth movements must be developed if we wish to provide a broader base for adult leadership in the next generation. One way to give shape or form to a youth organization is by focussing on a single aspect of its members' lives, seeing the other aspects in relation to this central theme. In Europe, Catholic youth movements have been built on scouting. In this country a youth does not put a pack on his back and set out for the weekend or long holiday. The All-American boy has his fielder's glove, his football jersey, or his dufflebag with basketball or bowling shoes. Here, Catholic youth movements have been built largely around the gridiron, diamond, or bowling alley, with the dance floor bringing in the other sex and filling out the social life. There is much that can be said for this apostolate. It develops a parish loyalty, builds up acquaintances and fellowship with Catholics, promotes Catholic marriages, encourages reception of the sacraments. Still, it seems that a Catholic youth movement should do something more, should address itself to the basic problems of society as they affect youth and openly aim at developing apostolic attitudes by positive and direct means.

Can high school students effectively reform the defective institutions of the teenage world? Is this not too big a bite for youngsters? Is it realistic to ask teens to make this approach the base of a youth movement? We must avoid two extremes in dealing with young people. The first is to write them off as incapable of any serious thinking about real problems. The second is to think that they alone can do the job. The truth lies in the middle. They can modify harmful social pressures by a thorough-going group analysis of these problems followed by action that is directed toward a solution, no matter how insignificant the action may seem. Young people are capable of grappling with king-size ideas. Cynics who think differently have no business dealing with youth.

In the United States the Sodality has been the dominant spiritual youth movement. Explicitly called Catholic Action by Pius XII, the Sodality in recent years has put increasing emphasis on the small-group method. Dedicated to our Blessed Lady, the Sodality stresses the building of a deep spiritual life in its members through adherence to a rule of life which includes daily Mass with Communion and mental prayer. Besides these spiritual exercises there are weekly meetings which include a checkup on spiritual progress and a discussion on some subject related to the apostolate. The Sodality has never dodged or straddled social issues such as segregation. While the emphasis is on personal spiritual development, there has been the recognition that spirituality cannot be separated from life. Individual moderators may have failed to see it this way, but the Sodality itself cannot be accused of having an ostrich-like view of man's life in the world.

To look at another youth movement, the Young Christian Students organization asserts in its literature that the reform of student institutions is the object around which the movement is built. Quoting from their literature: "The Young Christian Students is an apostolic organization of high school boys and girls who are trying through personal formation and organized social action to Christianize high school students' attitudes and environment, enshrine the ideals of Christ in the hearts and activities of the students, to investigate and help solve the factors inimical to Christian education in recreation, work and family life." They write long sentences and tackle mighty tasks.

If institutional change is to be more than a discussion, it must deal with real-life situations and terminate in action. The action must be designed to bring about a change in the institution. If youngsters, for example, agree that the Friday night dances are enjoyable, but many girls are dancing with each other because boys crowd in corners or monopolize a few girls, then the action to be taken is obvious. They must devise a way to keep the walls uncluttered.

If the group investigated the costs of dates and proms and found competition and rivalry in spending, then action could be taken that would reverse the trend. If the action taken was designed to go beyond the group and change the custom at its roots, then it would be an institutional action. It would be personal in that it would start with a change in their own attitude and practices and institutional in that it would help change the pattern or climate for all teenagers. If a cup of water given in the name of Christ is so important, how much more important an institutional action done in His name and affecting an entire community. The fact is that we seldom have the opportunity to give a cup of water to a thirsty person, so that we have to look around us to find an equivalent way to express love for our neighbor today. Teens helping teens live in a more wholesome atmosphere may well be the cup of water Our Lord wants from them to slake the thirst of His Mystical Body.

The question is often asked, "What type of student should we start with?" The answer is simple. We begin with those who have some desire to pursue the ends of the movement, which may be only vaguely outlined for them. In the school environment, the type which is more inclined to join a Catholic Action group is the boy or girl who is already participating in one or more extracurricular organizations. He may be a combination of honor roll student and athletic hero. The objection is then raised, "Why spend time saving the saved?" When a coach takes over a coaching assignment in a school he does not look for the most anemic, the smallest, and least coordinated. He feels he can best spend his time developing those who already show promise.

At long last in the academic world educators are becoming increasingly concerned with the devastating waste of the talents of the gifted child. Special schools and special courses are being arranged lest the nation's greatest resource, intellectual genius, continue to lie fallow. Only in the last half of the fifties has the Church in the United States searchingly questioned its intellectual contribution to the country. Ellis, Weigel, Murray, Cavanaugh, Cogley and Rooney have been directing this soul-searching analysis of the failure of the Church in America to take its place in the mainstream of American intellectual life. We have been guarding our intellectual heritage of the centuries instead of sharing and developing it. Ours has been a custodial operation.

The Young Christian Students, without confining themselves to the high I.Q. group, have always seen that there is an intellectual apostolate to which Catholic youths with the necessary ability should address themselves. The degree to which a particular group will develop an intellectual program will depend on the chaplain or religious assistant and the capability of the group. Within the framework of a Catholic Action movement there should be much room for a variety of approaches and experimentation. There are no magic formulas.

The assistant in a parish is often at wits' end trying to devise a program that will hold his teenagers together in a parish youth organization. He may feel that a priest-directed program of sports and socials is an unfruitful use of priestly talent. He may want to develop young apostles from both his public and Catholic high school students. Experiments have been started on the parish level with Young Christian Students. Vincent Giese's *Patterns for Teenagers* describes one such attempt. The parish-centered Young Christian Students group has the possibility of attracting a wider variety of teenagers. On the parish level there is less of the authoritarian atmosphere which is necessary for an orderly school operation. But the parish assistant is a busy man. Youth organizations are only one facet of his apostolate. In some parishes where the Christian Family Movement has been in existence a few years, the parish priests are encouraging couples to act as stand-ins for the busy priest. These couples open their homes to the teens for the meetings. With their experience in the family apostolate they are qualified guides in most aspects of a youth movement. If the parish priest works closely with the couples and has also direct contact with the members of the parish YCS, there is the hope of real development of youth along apostolic lines.

What has been written in this chapter is merely an indication of trends or experiments in the youth apostolate. There is little satisfaction among Catholic youth leaders in the country that adequate organizations and programs have been developed. There is seldom anything tangible to point to as the result of apostolic youth organizations. Ultimately, the greatest changes will be in the attitudes of the membership rather than in the teenage institutions. No rod has been devised for the measuring of change in attitudes. The unheralded and selfless task of molding youth along apostolic lines will go on by those who have confidence in youth. Apostolic men will be formed from young rowdy rebels and mature Christian women from giddy girls. The fashioners of youth will receive their laurels in another world.

CHAPTER IX

The Downtown Apostolate

THE TRAIN STOPPED at a suburban station outside London. As I stepped from the train I quickly surveyed the area. The architecture of the buildings seemed to repeat that of a typical Chicago North Shore suburb. I was on my way to the parish church to celebrate my first evening Mass on the Feast of Corpus Christi, which is a holyday in England. The pastor was not a typical suburban pastor. He was eager to talk about what he called his "dormitory" parish. He questioned why he should do more than provide liturgical services for his parishioners since the parish was not the center of their lives.

He felt that it was the social institutions outside the parish that shaped their lives and that he was powerless against the effects of these institutions. He was merely reflecting the thought of Hertzler, in *Social Institutions,* who says, "the dominance of institutions is so effective and subtle that the indi-

113

viduals may flatter themselves that they are exercising their own sovereign wills, whereas, in reality, they are reflecting institutional fiat. They are so conditioned by institutional stimuli that they do not realize how their thinking, their will, and their overt behavior is controlled and fabricated."

In our society, the dominant institution is not the parish, it is occupational life or the economic institution. My friend also took a dim view of the family as the place to begin a change in the entire social order. In fact, this was his precise point in referring to his parish as a dormitory parish. To him, home is a place where people change their clothes, not their lives. Why work with families whose young people will marry and live in another parish? How could he ever create a real apostolic community with such mobility? Mobility was immobilizing this pastor.

His position stood in sharp contrast to the naive, often-expressed attitude of "if only every family made their home into a Christian sanctuary, then the world's problems would disappear." Although I did not entirely agree with the extreme view of this pastor, he did make a point that has been almost forgotten in the complacent fifties.

In the past people spent their whole day within the community where they lived—they worked, played, studied, and carried on their other activities there. But today most Americans divide their time between two different types of communities—the functional and the geographic. The functional community represents the network of associations which people form based on their role or function in society, particularly their occupational role; for example, retail store owners, dentists, auto workers, entertainers, and salesmen. The geographic community is based on a plot of ground, the family, the parish, and neighborhood. Modern city planners usually zone one area for residences and another for industry. Man's work and family are separated, not by chance, but by the design of our city fathers and man's desire for green grass.

The Church has based its parish structure on the geographic community. It establishes parishes where people live, not where they work. But how is the Church to influence the work communities in Chicago's Loop or New York's Manhattan? How is the Church to bring Christian principles to bear on the men in our city halls and state capitols—the men and women whose work is in political life? Seldom does the parish influence economic and political life. Rooted in the geographic community, the parish normally cannot bridge the gap between it and the functional community. Since parishes are established where people live, except for occasional devotional churches, the downtowns of America—the centers of our civilization—are wildernesses in the Church's parochial structure. Is the Church to make the Merchandise Mart, the Empire State Building, or the Pentagon a parish?

There is no question, however, about the Church's awareness of the problem at the top level. "Let us always take careful note of the fact that most of the great social problems which Catholics must face from now on, both in regard to their particular nature and their solutions, extend far beyond the restricted organizations of the parish," wrote Milan's Cardinal Montini, when he was Vatican Pro-Secretary of State.

Pope Pius XII said, "It must be remembered that notwithstanding the importance of the work that can be carried out in a parish and nowhere else, and the fundamental and irreplaceable energies of the parish, the rapidly growing complexity of modern life from a technical and spiritual point of view calls for a wider extension of Catholic Action."

In America, the Church has recognized that there are some

functions which cannot be adequately performed by the parish. The parish high school has given way in many cases to the central Catholic high school. The Catholic college and the Catholic hospital have never been parochial institutions. On a lay organizational level, the parish has never been the center for all Catholic organizations: the Knights of Columbus, the Foresters, Daughters of Isabella are examples. In our large dioceses there is an increasing proportion of diocesan priests assigned each year to non-parochial tasks. This turn of events may be regretted as a loss of function or importance for the parish. On the other hand, an analysis of the situation might show that many of the specialized and centralized functions these priests perform were never conceived as parochial responsibilities in the first place.

The change can be seen on the level of voluntary Church organizations. The fact that, according to Fichter, only 4 per cent of the parishioners are active in parish activities does not mean that 96 per cent are not participating in some Church organizations. While urban life has been becoming more complex, with neighborhood and local communities tending to lose importance, Catholic organizations are growing apace on city-wide diocesan and national levels. This should not be interpreted to mean that the members of supraparochial units are defecting from their parish, but that they are responding to a genuine and wider need.

In our large northern cities we have Catholic interracial councils. They answer the need Catholic laymen have to work on the racial problem on a city-wide basis. The problem of racial discrimination in the school system, in the hospitals and in job situations must be faced on the top levels where city-wide policies are formed. Likewise, the Catholic labor school movement which developed out of the depression and the rapid widespread organization of workers can no longer be operated effectively as a parish undertaking. It must start and remain on a city level in order to draw sufficient numbers and a competent faculty.

In addition to organizations that are affiliated with the Church on a diocesan or city-wide level are those civic and economic groups in which the full living of Christianity in the world demands that one take part. Trade unions, professional and business associations, civic and political organizations, highly specialized groups such as the Alcoholics Anonymous, are a few. Membership in these groups takes up time that otherwise might be given to a parish organization. If it is a choice between one of the above and a parish society, the ultimate decision must be based on how the Christian can best further the work of the Mystical Body. It is not expected that in every case the decision will be in favor of the parish society. Parish loyalty, narrowly conceived, cannot be the sole criterion of the fervent Catholic. The Christian in the world has a responsibility to the temporal order which might, in given cases, take priority over his responsibility to parish groups.

This poses an interesting question. Can a good Catholic be a poor parishioner? Can a good parishioner be a poor Catholic once he leaves the precincts of neighborhood, parish, and home? Can we expect people who assume responsibilities in the economic or political order which involve the common good and demand an almost around-the-clock dedication to belong to parish organizations? Such cases demand individual solutions, but they illustrate the possibility of a saintly Catholic being active as a parishioner only to the extent that he participates in liturgical services when he can and contributes to the support of his pastor. Then there is the Catholic professional man who is an editor of a Catholic magazine, or has a staff job with a diocesan or national organization which keeps him writing or speaking for the Church to the point that he has no time for his own Holy Name Society. While they are not the pillars of the parish, they may be the pillars of the Church and state. The failure to see it this way is the result of a parochialism that equates the parish with the total work of the Mystical Body.

This point about the layman's non-parochial duties could be construed as being divisive to the parish and the Christian family. Actually, both the parish and the family must see the layman in the totality of his life. Any segmented view that leaves out the major influence on the life of an individual or a family can only be a disservice to the Church. The layman must look beyond the horizons of his parish borders to the legislative assemblies, the halls of justice, and the marts of trade to complete his apostolate. On the other hand, I did have reservations about the London pastor's approach. Above all, I disagreed with his pessimism about training people for the downtown apostolate.

Regardless of the limitations of the parish, it must assume some responsibility for training parishioners for the downtown apostolate. A beginning can be made in the rectory. Once the priest has an awareness of the necessity for lay people to embrace the occupational and political institutions as an integral part of the restoration of all things in Christ, he will see opportunities for bringing the laity to see that they have a mission in these phases of the temporal order.

Without becoming an economist or labor-management expert, the priest can develop a sensitivity for work-life problems. "It is for the priest to hear the sirens sounding from the factories, those temples of technical achievement where the modern world lives and breathes," wrote Cardinal Montini. This sensitivity can be sharpened for the priest by an occasional visit to the major industrial plants of the area and by conversation with articulate parishioners who sit on both sides of the bargaining table. With this understanding, the priest's Sunday sermons will be studded with references to work-life that will establish rapport with the adults and help them see the link between work-life and redemption.

Obviously, the parish should go further in its concern for a just social order than the casual remarks of a sympathetic clergy. The parish organizations should mirror the Church's concern for a better world. Holy Name organizations could stimulate the thinking of the membership and bolster attendance with talks by experts on the urgency of social reform and individual areas of local concern. The fact that a subject is controversial should not deter the leadership. A debate on the right-to-work laws, or on differing methods of urban renewal, could be presented. Our Catholic organizations have been so long open to the special pleader that it might take time to establish an atmosphere of give-and-take wherein matters are not necessarily resolved at a particular meeting, but a clearer picture is unfolded.

Catholic Women's organizations have at their command tremendous resources for unfolding the Catholic social doctrine through their membership in the National Council of Catholic Women. The NCCW offers to diocesan councils a distillation of the best thinking of the Church on modern social problems. The biennial resolutions of the NCCW Congress are a summary of the best social thought in the Church today. Its National Committee on Social Action offers literature and suggestions which, if studied and acted on, would change the face of the American Church in the eyes of men.

Catholic women's organizations should follow the advice of Pope Pius XII and face up to the great changes in the role of women in the modern world. It is hardly within the province of the priest to dictate the direction which the women should take. He can do no more than proclaim from the pulpit the dignity of womanhood and restate the principles involved, which have been set down in the address of Pius XII on "Woman's Duties in the Social and Political Life." Ultimately, it will depend on the Catholic woman herself to set in motion changes and attitudes that will embody the principles. This task cannot be done by women individually, since they are already enmeshed in the system and are looking for the answers. There must be groups of women who are continually rethinking these changes in terms of the Gospel and papal documents.

Young people starting to work need on-the-job training in the Christian life, training that no school is equipped to give. This must be done against the background of their education, neighborhood, parish life, and family relations, as well as their associations in work. To shut out any facet of life is to stunt the growth of our youth apostolate. The Young Christian Workers, which is organized along parish lines, makes such an attempt. The YCW unquestionably works with the best age group if one views the movement as a training ground for the reconstruction of the social order. It gives youth vision and staying power for the later years when he comes to a position of influence in society. Through their annual national and regional conventions these young people assimilate the papal principles on a just social order in a way that is practical and intelligible. On the priest's part, it demands not expert knowledge but a genuine sympathy for the outside-the-parish problems of his parishioners. It is also a high tribute to youth to regard them as capable of a deeper attachment to the Church than that involved in patronizing of Catholic dances, ball games, beach parties, and picnics. YCW offers these, too, but as fringe benefits.

What can the family movements do about repressing such evils of the social order as racial discrimination, bad housing and urban decay, inflation and recessions, pockets of poverty, over-organization of government, lack of organization along industry council lines in economic life? What can the family movements do about creating a temporal order that is in keeping with Christian principles? There is no question that the family is concerned with and affected by it. This problem was brought home for me in a visit to one of Harlem's thriving Catholic parishes. Here is a people involuntarily sealed off from the rest of society, where better jobs are closed to them because of color; where crowded housing conditions create family tensions and force children to live their lives on the streets, except for bedtime; where hygiene and moral problems flow from these circumstances as day follows night. In a situation where husbands must hold two jobs and wives one in order to pay exorbitant rents, we must expect a high rate of marital problems in the form of divorce, common-law marriages, illegitimacy and crime. If the ingredients are present, the results must inexorably follow.

There are certain conditions necessary for family life the absence of which can only mean wholesale family disintegration. The family needs space, it needs the presence of all its members, particularly the one who holds the place of authority, it needs a family identity maintained through family customs and beliefs. But basically, the Harlem problem is not a family or geographic problem as much as it is a functional one which defies boundaries and cuts across all institutions of society. The problem is not simply one of more prayers and religious practice, as desirable as these may be. The restoration of family life means destruction of segregation as an institution, destruction of homes that are beyond rehabilitation, the limitation of the density of the area to the point that the people can breathe fresh air and move in an apartment without fraying each other's nerves. It means opening job opportunities in all categories of work, creating integrated housing patterns where people of both races are free to move in or out.

Subjects related to the economic order such as the right-to-work laws, unions, and the United Nations have been the topics of family movement inquiries. These matters are related to the home, and certainly can be defended as belonging in a family program. But because of the wide interests and background of the family groups and the span of subjects affecting the home, the economic aspect of life is only one phase to be considered. Programs dealing only with economic life can hardly be expected to bring actions that change matters at the roots. Wider discussion by family groups is invaluable in opening minds, creating a climate, and preparing people for a more specialized apostolate in more limited fields. The family movement, at least in its present state of development, is not adequately geared to assume responsibility for restoration of the entire fabric of the social order.

Often Catholic organizations, in their efforts to translate the Christian life into actuality, are exposed to the temptation to descend upon the corner druggist whom they see as a villain hiding behind a rack of paperbacks and comic books with lurid covers. We give the same kind of treatment to the theatre which affronts us by showing condemned pictures or to TV programs that offend our Catholic sensibilities. The reaction to our pressure varies all the way from complete cooperation to rigid opposition. Pressure tactics are usually legitimate but not always prudent or effective. They can range from economic boycott to congratulatory letters to the TV station for programs which suit the tastes of the group.

Whether the tactic is positive or negative, it is a consumer approach, and this is not the most effective way of changing an

institution. Why? Simply because the consumer is an outsider
and is limited to a geographic area. He has no internal function within the particular communication industry. Those who
have taken part in campaigns to stop Sunday shopping know
how ineffective the consumer approach is. Letters from bishops,
pulpit announcements, and resolutions of parish societies are
never as effective as the meetings of a trade association in a
smoke-filled room. It is in the union hall, the trade association
buildings, and the cocktail lounges that economic policy and
opinions are formulated. These are the places where the decisions so vitally affect the family and where the family as an
institution or an apostolate is so completely unable to fend for
itself. It is the economic order that tells a man where he can
afford to live, how much education his children can obtain, and
what opinions to hold in business life and politics. It is the people in these functional categories who will make whatever
changes are needed. The downtown area of our cities cries out
for an apostolate. The larger issues of society must be changed
ultimately by people involved in the making of them rather than
by pressure groups from the outside.

Both the clergy and the laity can act as a pressure group.
Since both are consumer groups, they can with equal voice ask
the local druggist to clean up his magazine rack. The layman
and the priest have in the past teamed up in this militant but
negative approach to social action. Has a Communist infiltrated
a government office, has a secular university failed to respect
the rights of a Catholic chaplain, is there an American priest in
a Communist camp, has PAOU baited us again? We need cru-
saders to defend our vested interests, but we have a more urgent need for people who, without flamboyant oratory, will
work to repair the sinking ship, people who, without a partisan

approach, will devote themselves to untangling the skein of civil liberties for all groups and individuals.

The city with its noise, its nervous pace, its factory chimneys belching soot, its brightly lighted marquees, its five-star final, its paper-shuffling and filing cabinets, its Madison Avenue approach to sales, its ticker tape that records the cycles of prosperity and depression, must come under the redeeming influence of Christ, through the layman. Here the clerically motivated and family-centered pressure group is hopelessly inadequate.

The layman must act as a layman here on his own responsibility and see in this commitment to lay life a path of sanctity. If Christ has a stake in what happens in one's occupational life, the layman cannot be indifferent to it. He cannot shirk responsibility because he has a family and has membership in Catholic organizations. There is no set of rules which determine in a particular case whether an occupational apostolate, a family apostolate or a parish society has priority. It is the narrow view that sees any devotion to occupational organizations at the expense of parish organizations as a defection from full Catholic life. Such a view stems from a failure to understand the Christian's responsibility for social action. It is true that the Church has no mission to direct the temporal order, although she may and should have an influence upon the economic, political and intellectual movements of our day. While the Church does not become involved in technical concerns and does not endorse a particular political party, it urges its lay members to establish their citizenship in the City of Man by genuine involvement. The failure of the layman to embrace the temporal order is an implicit denial of the Incarnation and Redemption, and also evidences a taint of Manicheism.

The responsibility of the Christian for social action has been well-expressed by de Montcheuil: "There are forms of government which either hinder or favor the awareness of the individual person of his own worth, which either guarantee or subjugate his rights. . . . The communion of individuals will be perfectly achieved only in heaven, but the Christian who sincerely desires communion with God cannot fail to begin to desire it on earth and to work for it as much as possible. Looking at all institutions, he asks himself whether or not they hinder the communion of individual men, a communion which he will never really find perfect enough either in depth or breadth. Therein lies a principle of action for the Christian for, although only a miserable, rough outline of the heavenly city can be achieved here below, the Christian never wearies of trying to make it less imperfect."

Just as in the sphere of the family the Church's view of man's nature and his destiny form a pattern of social values that must be implemented and preserved through family-action programs, so in the economic and political sphere the Church's view of man has been elaborated for us by papal teaching and demands implementation through action groups. Social action movements are the answer of the Church to the ideologies and social problems flowing from the Industrial Revolution and from the unprecedented growth of the human family.

Social action movements cannot be blueprinted. Nor do the actions that obtain results in one country necessarily have validity in another. As in other phases of the lay apostolate, the approach to social action movements must be a problematic or pragmatic one. One of the first questions that must be asked is whether Catholic professional or occupational groups are desirable. There is no question about one's responsibility to a profession or occupation, but perhaps we should establish an intermediate Catholic group that mediates between the individual Catholic and the secular occupational group. In more concrete terms, should we establish Catholic guilds for lawyers, doctors, postal workers, policemen, and the whole gamut of career and job categories? There are two objections. The effectiveness of the commitments a man already has in secular life might be prejudiced by active membership in another organization. Secondly, the effectiveness of a Catholic in the temporal order will be in proportion to his ability to work with people of other faiths in secular organizations. Would his participation in a Catholic occupational group have a divisive effect? Would the Catholic organization create a "Catholic block"?

Certainly, Catholic lay people contemplating organizing or joining occupational groups must honestly answer these questions. They should ask, "Why another group?" If the function of the group is merely to provide proof of numerical strength and organizing ability to members and outsiders, then the group could hardly be justified. If the purpose is to promote a corporate reception of Holy Communion and hear a speech on the evils of the day, it seems to be encroaching upon the family and the parish without reason. The Catholic occupational group is justified when it inquires into the status of its members in the temporal order to see where their work deviates from Christian teaching and to explore the possibilities of the members making a greater contribution to their professional and occupational life. In actuality, Catholics often work at cross purposes with the Pope, if we compare their actions or statements with papal statements on the same subject. In brief, another Catholic organization can only be justified if it is geared to helping the membership make a greater contribution to the occupation or profession itself.

Are these organizations conducive to "Catholic blocks"? A certain amount of hostility is unleashed by anything Catholic.

This we discount because of its unreasonableness. However, if a Catholic organization respects the general norms of Catholic Action, the individual members act in the temporal order not as representatives of Catholic Action and, therefore, not as spokesmen for the Church, but as individual Christians who ask a hearing because of their competency and citizenship in their occupation. A Catholic "block" is utterly repugnant to Catholics in the field of social action. Europe offers examples of the sad consequences of people aligning according to denomination on temporal matters. A Catholic "block" in temporal affairs is divisive because it looks askance upon and inhibits cooperation with people of other faiths. Psychologically it is a defense for feelings of inadequacy. Actually, solutions to social problems in a pluralistic society can only come from the consensus of people of many faiths. This is in keeping with the best traditions of the American Church.

We cannot blueprint or call into being social movements, but on the basis of the experiments and currents of thought abroad, we can do some crystal-gazing. We envision a dominantly lay social action movement working at many levels. First, on a city-wide basis, involving people in a particular trade or occupation, such a movement could bring Catholic members of trade associations together to analyze common problems as a guide to action. Small groups of union officials could likewise meet to assess collectively the Christian implications of their work. Such meetings could be extended to the professions and the other categories of people in the occupational world. Each group could choose its own structure for meetings and procedure. Two elements, however, seem necessary. There should be some spiritual orientation to the group if it is to be apostolic. This could be done through an occasional evening of recollection, but more important would be a discussion of the

problem, which would be akin to the social inquiry, and a pur-
suant action—the essence of Catholic Action. There must be
more than a mere lecture series to qualify as social action.

A second level of operation would be groupings of specialists to solve wider community problems. Many problems in the
economic order are not simply those of a single industry or of
one segment of the economy, but involve the entire complex
of industrial life. Urban redevelopment programs are an example. No longer is good housing a matter of the individual concern of the home owner; the stability of a neighborhood depends
on the collective action of the people. Ordinarily, a blighted
area cannot be restored without a community organization and
the assistance of a number of governmental agencies.

Urban redevelopment requires human relations committees
to give experience and help in handling the racial problem involved in relocating people. Bankers, insurance companies, real-
tors, architects, builders, church and school officials, all must
be brought into the endeavor. An effective social action group
in the field of housing would need to include a wide array of
specialists to cope with all the dimensions of what seems like a
simple domestic problem. A Catholic social action group in the
field of housing needs more than a group of people of good will.
It needs competency as much as it needs dedication.

World problems are included in the scope of a social action
movement. The world population problem has put the Catholic
on the defensive in regard to his stand on birth control. It is not
enough for him to say that artificial birth control is an offense
against nature and in the long run can only bring destruction
upon the human race. The fact that two-thirds of the people of
the world live in over-populated or underdeveloped areas where
food shortages are the normal condition, plus the prospects of
further population explosions, demands more than a parrot-like

response about the natural law. We must think creatively about world organizations that study population and food problems, foreign aid programs, and technical as well as financial assistance to missions.

Unfortunately, a dry spell that burns the front lawn, the late delivery of the milk in a bad storm, or a burnt piece of toast for breakfast, are greater tragedies to many people than the fact that in the large Oriental cities police pick up every morning corpses of people who died on the street during the night because of lack of food and shelter. A dollar in a collection basket for the Bishops' Relief Fund is a good way out for most people who should be thinking seriously about the political, economic and technical problems involved in wiping hunger from the face of the earth. A social action movement can be selfishly and exclusively concerned with pay raises, longer vacations and other fringe benefits—which indeed have contributed to the American way of life; while there are Koreans hungry and Japanese naked, the social actionist, and all of us, are called upon for a deeper involvement.

A third level of a social action movement would be in the form of an Academy of Catholic Social Thought which would be an unofficial spokesman on social problems. Its influence would be based on the prestige of its members and the clarity of their argument. It seems that a social action movement, if it is organized and coordinated and has within its ranks university professors as well as technical experts, should be able to create a body of Catholic opinion on social problems. The right-to-work laws furnish an example. The promoters of these laws claim that they will protect the right of freedom of association for the individual. Their adversaries claim that they will destroy existing harmonious relationships between employer and employees. The judgement of the morality of these laws must be based on an analysis of American labor-management practices. One's view, therefore, will be colored by his experiences, with the result that people of good-will will find themselves in opposite camps.

On such disputed questions people look to authorities for guidance in forming their judgements. In the case of the right-to-work laws, a number of bishops in scattered parts of the country, plus the bishops of Ohio and the overwhelming majority of priests interested in social action, have declared themselves opposed to the laws. There was a consensus of Catholic thought on this subject, despite the fact that a few well-known priests took positive stands to the contrary; but the Church, and the individual bishops, had no intention of binding all Catholics to a single opinion.

While priests, as guardians of the moral law and as citizens, can and should take a stand on the side which the evidence leads them to embrace as true, it seems that the Church would be better served if there was a Catholic social action organization, predominantly lay in composition and competent in its field, to express an opinion which could be weighed on its merits without committing the Church. The point at issue here is not the right of bishops and priests to speak on social problems, but on what to speak, how frequently, and in what manner.

The Church's Magisterium should not be involved in every turn of social events, but a reputable body of scholars and experts could be a guide to action. Who speaks for the Church, and when does it speak, are questions that need clarification for the Church in America. The problem can be seen clearly in the Catholic Press. When the editor of a diocesan paper writes an editorial, is he expressing an opinion which demands no more acceptance than the reasons supporting it? Or is the

editor expressing the mind of the bishop, since the paper is his
official news organ, and does the editor thereby command the
obedience of the bishop's subjects, since the bishop has spoken
through him? The Catholic Press Association grapples with this
problem in its annual meetings. In our democratic type of society, maturity can only be developed in Catholic laity by allow-
ing them as much freedom as possible to form opinions and
debate issues, with Catholic social principles as a common base.

Walter Lippman, in *The Public Philosophy,* states the problem of any religious group arriving at a consensus on a practical issue:

> In the immediate, urgent and particular issues of daily life the
> major prophets, the seers, and the sages, have remarkably little to
> offer by way of practical advice and specific guidance. The de-
> posit of wisdom in the Bible and in the classic books does not
> contain a systematic and comprehensive statement of moral prin-
> ciples from which it is possible to deduce with clarity and cer-
> tainty specific answers to concrete questions. He who goes to this
> wisdom looking for guidance of this sort will be disappointed. If
> he finds it there, he must come to it by analogy and by inference.
> The specific rules of conduct are not explicitly there. Were they
> there, the history of mankind would have been different. For
> terrible wars and poisonous hatreds arise among men who draw
> irreconcilably different practical conclusions from the same gen-
> eral principles. There is a hiatus between the highest wisdom
> and the actual perplexities with which men must deal.

Religiously orientated groups may have their limitations in
speaking on public issues, but they must keep a dialogue alive
on these subjects if the teachings of Christ and His Church are
to take flesh in the institutions of the City of Man.

Catholic social movements are the response of the Church to
the vast changes in our technological era which gave such importance to the functional community. The famous sermons,

"The Great Social Questions of Our Times," by Bishop von Kettler in Mainz, Germany, in 1848, marked the beginning of these movements. In this country the first steps can be traced to Monsignor Ryan of Washington, D. C. Since John A. Ryan's background was in moral theology and economics, the result was that social action became associated with economic action. In Canada, the movement fits more closely the sociologist's definition of social action by including in its structure the family and youth apostolates. In this country, the clerical side of the Church has dominated the social action movement. To its glory, it has given us the so-called "labor," and "waterfront" priests of the thirties and forties.

The fact that the social action movement has been concerned with the economic institutions and has been clerical in personnel and approach can be defended on theological and historical grounds. The direction it should take today has been opened for debate by Monsignor Ryan's successor, Monsignor George G. Higgins, the present director of the Social Action Department of the NCWC. In 1955, after a lapse of sixteen years, the Department began to sponsor annual conferences for priests and laity actively involved in social action throughout the country. The theme of the 1957 conference—"Changing Social Action in a Changing World"—was significant of the state of the movement. Out of the 1958 discussion has come the National Catholic Social Action Conference, which is a permanent organization whose members are both clerical and lay, and are engaged in social action in this country. A layman was elected first president.

On the grassroots level, practically every large city has a social action operation. There is little similarity in structure or type of services performed. In many cities labor-management schools are sponsored. In another the emphasis is upon publications, annual lecture series, and small-group meetings. While the social action operations on the grassroots level bring clergy and laity together in a wholesome and profitable relationship, with lay responsibility being delegated and accepted, the movement—with notable exceptions—remains a clerical movement. This author sees it as a necessary development for our social action movement to change from a clerical operation to a lay movement, if social action is to flower as an effective apostolate in the economic order. The alternative is to become exclusively an adult education movement in the field of Catholic social principles.

The Catholic social action movement in this country is just drawing its second wind. The necessity of work in this area has long been recognized and supported by the hierarchy. As Catholic Action movements and Catholic colleges create an awareness of the institutional apostolate, more laymen will regard the areas staked off by the social action movement as worthy of dedication. The precise direction the movement in the United States will take is not yet clear. The Holy Spirit working through the changing circumstances of history will chart the course.

CHAPTER X

Spirituality for the Laity

W HETHER OR NOT there is such a thing as lay spirituality seems to be a matter of semantics. There is only one Christian life which stems from a single source. The Christian life flows from the open side of Christ on the Cross. It is the same divine life which is shared by Trappist and truck driver. We can think of the Christian life flowing from the side of Christ into different types of lives. We can compare it to molten iron being poured into different molds. The molds may all be different in size and unlike in every way, but the substance in them is the same. So with the Christian life. The mold is shaped by the circumstances of daily life. Into it is channelled the divine life, the Christ-life, or what is traditionally called sanctifying grace.

Generally speaking, the people who write and talk about spirituality for the laity are reacting against the layman being

134

treated as a second class citizen when it comes to having the full Christian ideal of sanctity or perfection presented to him.

The people who have pioneered in this subject have noted that the books given to devout lay people were written, with the exception of the *Devout Life* of St. Francis de Sales, for priests and religious. Some lay organizations have been presented as extensions of the religious life, as though lay life could not be an authentic way of life. The parish-mission preacher is apt to talk dourly on the single and married states of life in negative terms of duty and obligation, rather than in terms of a vocation to holiness. This all adds up to a low esteem for the layman's capacity for holiness.

It is quite possible to exaggerate the difference between the lay saint and the saintly priest or religious. Both will excel in charity, both practice patience, humility and the long categories of Christian virtues. Quite conceivably, the theologians will finally agree that there are no essential differences between the spiritualities of a layman and a priest, that the differences are what the philosophers call accidents. Nevertheless, these differences are presently considered important enough for there to be separate retreats for priests, religious, married couples, single adults, and teenagers. The layman's life needs to be examined within the framework of these accidental differences to explore the possibilities of sanctity and the shape our times demand this sanctity take.

One Sunday evening I intruded upon a meeting of a dozen diocesan priests who had gathered to discuss spirituality for the laity. Although they were quite capable of an academic discussion of the subject, they were practitioners who labored every day at the task of forming Christ in people who work for a living. They were quite aware of the almost uncharted theological field that this subject is opening up and the beginnings made by

Congar in his *Lay People in the Church*, but they did not want to get bogged down on this particular facet of theology. The meeting was designed simply for the pooling of resources and experiences that gives to each a broader view of the task and keeps him from pressing one approach exclusively.

At a previous meeting, they had set the stage by forming an ideal concept of a parish: "It is a parish in which a dominant group of people are: (1) acutely conscious of religion in their everyday life; (2) realize that they are cooperating with the other members of the parish in a joint struggle to gain heaven (common goal); (3) are constantly trying to improve intellectually (knowledge of God) and spiritually (practice of virtue); and (4) have a sense of community worship at Mass."

The group further defined the ideal Catholic as "one who has a dynamic awareness of the Mystical Body worshipping and transforming the world of men and things; one who, as father, husband, worker, student, etc., is exercising himself as a Christian in all these areas of his life." What must the parish, and in particular the parish priest, do to help people achieve this ideal? That was the problem discussed. It was a "how to do it" meeting. The meeting was lively and stimulating enough to get this writer to use it as a springboard to order his thoughts on the subject.

I suppose there are some people who fit this description of an ideal Catholic yet have not had the special help of a spiritual guide, a liturgy-orientated parish, or membership in an apostolic movement. They get it, as it were, by osmosis. It may have been an aside from a teacher, or a casual conversation that led them to read Bloy, Maritain and others; this, combined with docility to the promptings of the Holy Spirit, set them in motion. Such specially gifted people are rare. We are, therefore, setting down a five-pronged program for the rank and file Catholic. They are not necessarily successive stages, nor are they neat compartments since a person can be involved in all of them at the same time.

The first step is to get people to wet their feet apostolically. Billy Graham is never satisfied with merely thrilling an audience with an electrifying speech and having them verbalize a few "Amens." He asks that they make "decisions for Christ," whereby they openly disclose their allegiance for Christ by stepping out of the crowd and making a public declaration of intention. With Billy this is a first and necessary step. It is an initial commitment to Christ.

Priests involved in developing lay people for the apostolate use no dramatic appeal like Billy's in seeking commitments for Christ. They begin by trying to get people involved in doing something for Christ, no matter how unsensational it might be. In the beginning, explanations and reasons are not as important as action.

The apostolic feet-wetting process is an application of the Dewey philosophy of "learning by doing." I remember listening to a group of high school sophomores in a YCS meeting sweat over the sentence, "If any man wishes to be first among you, he shall be last of all and servant of all." They spent fifteen minutes vainly trying to find an application to their lives. The next morning one of them left the cafeteria breakfast table an unsightly mess. I started to clean up myself in the presence of one of the offenders who had also been present the evening before. I simply stated that this is what last night's Gospel meant.

Another week we discussed our Lord's washing the feet of the apostles. To initiated Christians, it stands for fraternal charity. For the uninitiated, the meaning is far from obvious. They must laboriously spell it out themselves in terms of concrete situations at recreation, at school, at home. They must experience the joy of doing something for somebody without an ulterior motive.

Another way of describing the feet-wetting process is in terms of involvement. Involvement is the principle of the professional fund-raisers. More important than urging a person to write a check for a good cause is to ask him to be a worker for the cause, to ask him to contact others about check-writing. Experience proves that the worker's personal monetary contribution will be increased by the fact that he becomes involved as a worker. The greatest dignity that can be conferred upon a person is to give him the opportunity to give of his very substance.

Some sociologists of religion claim that common beliefs are what unite a people. We are united, they say, when we hold a common system of values that reach the deepest issues of our lives and determine our code of right and wrong. This view does not seem complete. People must not only believe, but they must become involved in the implications of their belief. The belief must establish common endeavors that cement the beliefs into a shared way of life. Without these reciprocal relations, or involvement in meaningful actions, the beliefs will die. The difference between the living parish and the dormant parish is the quantity and quality of involvement of the parishioners in action. The same thing can be said of the difference between the nuclear Catholic and the marginal Catholic. The more a Catholic is involved, ordinarily, the deeper will be his faith.

While we start with involvement in an action or project, the involvement must in time take on the substance of a cause outside ourselves to which we devote ourselves unselfishly. This dedication can have a transforming effect upon the entire personality. Books on the spiritual life seldom treat this aspect. Too often they regard the person as a disincarnate spirit whose job is the arithmetical one of counting acts of virtue, of consciously building up a spiritual edifice, virtue by virtue. Dietrich von Hildebrand gives the lie to this approach in a masterful sentence. "It is not from what we undertake with a view to our transformation, but from the things to which we devote ourselves for their own sake, that will issue the deepest formative effect upon our habitual being." Obviously, it is the quality of unselfishness and dedication to others that gives involvement or commitment its transforming power. This quality of dedication is seldom present when one is in the feet-wetting process. One may come to a meeting to make new friends, because one is tired of TV, or for a multitude of selfish or indifferent reasons, but out of this can come real commitment. It is the necessary first step of an infant or of a person recovering from paralysis.

In a previous chapter, we have pointed to the urgency of an apostolate dedicated to the institutions beyond the parish and family, and pointed to the limitations of CFM and other apostolic groups for this type of operation. On the other hand, it is hard to conceive how these long-range institutional apostolates will ever develop unless there are groups like CFM who engage people in the apostolate at the feet-wetting level. If Sodalists, YCS, and other youth groups actively engage people in the apostolate of the Church, even at the level of teenage social life, they are giving them a sense of the mission of the Church by involving them in the work of the Church. This can be the seed for long-term dedication to an institutional apostolate of another generation.

St. John narrates the story of the man with a withered body who waited for the water in the pool to be stirred by the angel. The man never got to the water after the stirring simply because he had no one to carry him. There are many people whom the priest and dedicated laymen come in contact with who would want to be healed of their lethargy and give themselves to Christ through the use of their distinctive talents, if there were only someone to move them. There is no one to bring them to the waters to get their feet wet apostolically. The feet-wetting operation is a break-through after years of formalistic religious training and routine performance to the genuine religious experience wherein the beneficiary of our action is seen as Christ in the person of a fellow man.

The second approach is the "shock" treatment. The first method is slow and taxing on one's patience. The change is not evident immediately; there are no violent changes in one's way of life. The "shock" treatment is the thrusting of people into situations in which all the values of their life are brought into violent conflict. This is the treatment the Catholic Worker gave to people in the thirties. When people came to volunteer they were not given a six week indoctrination course, but rather a mop, or a dish cloth and a tub of dirty dishes.

This treatment is still used successfully in teaching the implications of the Mystical Body. The housing patterns of our large Northern cities indicate continued segregation to the point that two cities, one white and one Negro, are developing within the corporate limits of a single metropolis. An expert on race relations estimates that in the city of Chicago 98 per cent of the Negroes do not have a single face-to-face relationship with a white person as an equal. He also estimates that the converse is true, that 98 per cent of the whites do not have a Negro acquaintance in whom they can confide as an equal. This amounts to almost a complete deterioration of human relations.

Antipathies based on race are built into many people who have had only the slightest contact with members of another race. The antipathy may be aroused by no more than a brush in a subway or a bus and can result in behavior that borders on the pathological, if not overtly criminal. The first fully human contact between races often requires an individual to do near-violence to himself in overcoming his fears. Interracial centers like Friendship House provide the kind of shock people need. It offers its services in providing contacts with Negro and white people for Catholic high school students and YCW groups who have never visited a Negro family except in a paid service capacity. A Saturday spent climbing the stairs of broken down tenement buildings and sitting over a cup of coffee at a kitchen table can do for a youngster what a shelf of sociology textbooks, or even a Gospel discussion, could not do.

An invaluable experience of this type, one which can lead to a grasp of world problems, is the welcoming of a foreign student to one's home. Families have found their horizons immeasurably extended by an Indian or a Chinese student sitting at their table and telling the children of Oriental customs and teaching them geography, and at the same time subtly teaching the parents of America's international responsibility and Christ's stake in the lands of teeming millions.

Suburbanites have no reason to apologize because they like fresh air, green grass, and living space that affords some privacy. This was the vision of a better social order that many dedicated apostles advocated in the thirties and forties for the working people of America. The realization of the goal for hundreds of thousands of families must be considered a distinct gain. What bothers some is that when people have arrived, they forget their origins and lose interest in bringing these good things to the less fortunate. They might well meditate on the song of David, substituting "God's poor" for "Thee," "If I forget Thee, O Jerusalem, let my right hand be forgotten. Let my tongue cleave to my jaws, if I do not remember Thee." Creative thought must be given to means of retaining our social gains while maintaining our association with the poor, the lonely and the aged. The new middle class must be kept shockingly aware of the suffering of God's poor.

Spiritual guides and movements that aim at developing the Christian life among the laity must consider how to thrust people into situations where they are confronted with circumstances in which they feel uncomfortable. The Judgment scene where Christ identifies Himself with the hungry, thirsty, naked, sick and lonely must be anticipated in this life. Christ came to disturb us: "Do you think that I came to give peace upon the earth? No, I tell you, but division." He wants to take away our rocking chair and slippers and give us a restless concern for the less privileged. There is nothing that bares the soul and brings it face-to-face with Christ so much as the compassion we experience in binding and kissing the wounds of those whom contemporary society considers lepers. Not to have this shocking experience is a Christian's woe. A realistic concern for God's poor must be a normal phase of a layman's spiritual development.

The third prong of the program might seem at first to be the opposite of what the classical spiritual writers call the "conversion to God." It seems that our times call for a "conversion to the world," presuming that there has been a "conversion to God." It is interesting to see how lay people like to shy away from the world when they become re-converted to God. Too often they want to love God apart from the stock exchange, courts of justice, the factories, offices, or marts of trade that traffic in mundane and often sordid deeds. Too often they would rather have Gospel discussions, make Advent wreaths, send religious Christmas cards and limit their forensic skills and political acumen to a crusade against Communism and to sniping at the UN for its godlessness.

Because we have not developed a spirituality of work or

genuine respect for the temporal order as a path to holiness, there is in some quarters a distrust of created things. This is nothing new in Christianity. It can be traced to the Desert Fathers of the third century. The hermits of the desert days of early Christianity engaged in basket weaving. When they finished weaving the basket, they unwove it and did it over. While they worked, they contemplated. Work was only a means to an end, hardly a good in itself. In the novitiate of a religious community, novices are taught how to pray while working. On a rainy day, the novice master might make work to keep them busy. In this monastic view, work is not so much a value in itself as it is a tool of prayer. Out of this develops the spirituality of intention. Since it is only the intention that counts, work is of little value. The spirituality of intention is based on the fact that the Christian shares in the divine nature through grace, so that if he even picks up a pin and is motivated by the love of God his act has eternal reverberations. These insignificant actions have divine consequences whether we think about them or not. The morning offering takes care of the intention. The religious, too, because of a vow of obedience may be indifferent to the kind and type of work he does. The novice master may tell his charges that it is not sweeping a floor or teaching a class that is the important thing, but doing what one is told to do with love.

If the layman's spirituality is a trickle-down religious spirituality, there can be disastrous consequences. The layman, because he is a layman, must have a different view of work. In work life, he is paid for what he produces. Work puts a roof over the family and overtime puts a car in the garage. The perfection of the work itself counts with the layman. Faulty work may cripple the entire industry or endanger the lives of many people. Work has tremendous consequences for the layman that the religious may find difficult to appreciate. It might be said parenthetically that religious who teach, nurse or are engaged in the administration of these or other services must take the layman's view of work and achieve in these fields, as a very minimum, the competency of the lay leaders in these fields.

The layman must be taught not only to accept work as his lot in life, but to embrace it. Not merely to tolerate it, but to see in it his calling by God to complete the work of creation and to cooperate in the work of redemption. Each ton of coal mined, each shelter built completes what God left unfinished. The sweat and monotony of work, if joined to the bloody sweat of Christ offered in the Mass, continue the work of redemption. The toil and tears of work should be for the layman what St. Paul refers to as a filling up "of those things that are wanting to the sufferings of Christ." The layman must indeed offer up his work, but he must see that the work itself is important and that the nature and quality of it have an eternal importance simply because it is the substance of the temporal order for which he has the responsibility.

There will always be a tension between the demands of the temporal order and the needs of the spirit. Escape from the battle can never be justified. Basically, we are dealing with a failure of religiously motivated people to have a respect for the nature and truth of earthly things. In the word of Congar: "Lay people are called to the same end as clergy or monks—to the enjoyment of our inheritance as sons of God; but they have to pursue and attain this end without cutting down their involvement in the activities of the world, in the realities of the primal creation, the disappointments, the achievements, the stuff of history."

What we are trying to describe is what Ruth Nanda terms "a new style sanctity": "In these perspectives we may understand that a new style of sanctity, a new step in the sanctification of secular life, will be demanded by the new age. Not only will the spirit of Christ spread into secular life, seek for witnesses among those who labor in yards and factories, in social work, politics or poetry, as well as among monks dedicated to the search for perfection; but a kind of divine simplification will help people to realize that the perfection of human life does not consist in a stoical athleticism of virtue nor in a bookish and humanly calculated application of holy recipes, but rather in a ceaselessly increasing love, despite our mistakes and weaknesses, between the Uncreated Self and the created Self. There will be a growing consciousness that everything depends on that descent of the divine plenitude into the human being."

The motto of St. Pius X, "to restore all things in Christ," has long been a Catholic Action slogan. It is still an objective for people who tend to compartmentalize their lives and see their relations with God strictly in terms of religious acts. Work itself must become a way to God, not merely an interlude between morning and evening prayers. An authentic spirituality for the laity must aim at an integration of work and worship.

The fourth ingredient in the development of the ideal Catholic is community. Our Lord formed a community with His Apostles, and the early Christians attempted common life on a wide scale. Even the Desert Fathers gradually clustered around spiritual leaders like Anthony and Paul. Until recently, however, we associated Christian community with the religious life or the rural parish in Catholic countries where village, parish and kinship formed a single unit.

One of the most far-reaching changes in parish life came with the freedom of worship in democratic societies. The spires of Protestant churches in our communities means not only that Catholics are free to worship but that the parish community and the geographic community can no longer be forged into a single social unit. In our pluralistic society, community in this sense is no longer possible.

Today, we must face the reality that a big city parish community, like a big family, is sociologically impossible; the closest approximation would be the conception of the parish as a federation of smaller groupings. These lesser communities can be the training centers for developing and sustaining the "ideal Catholic." These sub-groupings may be informal meetings of friends who gather at irregular intervals to discuss some aspect of the Christian life. They can be highly organized, as the Legion of Mary, CCD or YCW. They may be school-based, parish-centered or city-wide. The groups may have elaborate training programs like the Grail, or shorter annual gatherings like NCCW institutions or study weeks, that gather the clan under one roof for common prayer, discussion, and recreation in order to cement the bonds of community.

Providing the initial spadework has been done, the group can do for each other what the priest and the individual accomplish through a dialogue. In these groups and larger meetings, there are immense possibilities for apostolic growth. Older people can play the role of counsellor for younger members on condition that the elders have gone through the above three stages. Group therapy is a recognized counselling art. It is, after all, a physical impossibility to have a priest present in every place where two or three people are gathered together in our Lord's name.

Father Spae, the Japanese missionary, is opposed to individual convert instructions on principal, and would permit them only by way of exception. He believes that the catechumen must learn from and with the group. Christians are not being brought into the Church to live isolated lives. They are coming into a living community. Every priest dealing with converts is aware of the frustration of the newly baptized person who has no family support for his new religion, and who likewise finds no community support through his contacts with the parish. The priest sees converts come enthusiastically in the front door and slide out the back door because of the lack of the sustaining power which only the community can give. Whether neophytes or seasoned Catholics, people can develop spiritually only through a community.

The fifth step is formal spiritual indoctrination. At the priests' meeting mentioned above, I was holding forth on the shock treatment when I was reminded that it was only one method, one piece in the puzzle. If involvement and the shock treatment were our total approach, we would be pursuing an American humanitarianism of "deeds not creeds." There must be a doctrinal framework for the apostle. This we shall develop in the next chapter.

I came away from the priests' meeting with what seems like an odd conclusion. Here were a dozen diocesan priests gathered to discuss a spirituality for the laity. Actually, what they were doing to a great extent was defining the role of the priest, and thus they were spelling out a distinct spirituality for diocesan priests.

CHAPTER XI

A View of the Apostolate

INCREASINGLY, lay Catholics are accepting the call to the apostolate. Usually the awakening to it comes through membership in an apostolic group. With commitment to the work of the group, comes the realization that Christianity is more than the sum of religious activities. It is a life. And with the consciousness that it is a life comes the deepening conviction that the life must be nourished.

The Christ-life must be fed upon Christ's words, as well as upon the Bread of the liturgy. While the life of Christ narrated by the Evangelist fills the reader with the grandeur and nobility of a human life lived most perfectly, it is not the most significant facet of the Christ-life for the Catholic. The moral teachings, parables, and examples in the life of Christ may overwhelm us as we read and meditate upon them, but the unimaginable reality of Christ's sharing His divine life with creatures is far more gripping. This must be the vital fact in the life of the neophyte lay apostle and the one given priority in his training.

We are called, not simply to share His mission, but His very life, as we go about our daily, routine chores. Christ says to each of us: "I have come that you may have life and have it more abundantly." Since we took possession of this abundant life at Baptism, we may have seldom reflected upon it except in terms of restoration through the sacrament of Penance. Christ's redemptive design for the human race is that all share His life.

Since Christ is the author and the Holy Spirit is the giver of divine life, man can only prepare the world for the diffusion of this life. An awareness of the doctrine of divine life should create an apostolic restlessness to remove all the personal and social barriers that impede the divinization of mankind. The apostle wants to identify himself with Christ and to share that abundant life, so that Christ can speak for each and say, "Behold, I make all things new."

The second doctrine that shapes the apostle and the apostolate is the Mystical Body. It is no coincidence that the exploration and the elaboration of the doctrine of the Mystical Body and the growth of the apostolate have been simultaneous. To many teachers of Christian doctrine the Mystical Body is like frosting on the cake. They feel that they never get to the point with people where they have exhausted the doctrinal approaches of the past century. It is with a sense of amazement that one picks up the new Killgallon-Weber *Life in Christ* catechism and finds that the divine life and the Mystical Body are presented without apology to the adult neophyte as initial approaches and the standard teaching for catechumens. It is more fascinating to find that lay people who are exposed to the truth of the Church in adult life often find less difficulty with these approaches than an older generation of teachers. These older teachers have been inhibited by the post-Reformation concept of the Church as a juridic entity founded by Christ, to the exclusion of a treatment of the mystery of God's union with men in the Mystical Body. Lay people whose thinking processes have not yet atrophied and who have this doctrine explained to them initially in simpler terms than in the encyclical on the Mystical Body find this doctrine an exhilarating experience. There is no satisfying this thirst once it is created.

The Mystical Body continues the triple role of Christ as Ruler, Priest and Teacher. The theology of the nature and degree of sharing or participation of the laity in each of these three offices leaves much room for development. The power to rule in the Church belongs, in the strict sense, only to the Holy Father and the Bishops directly, but also in a real sense to priests duly ordained and authorized. There is a long tradition in the Church for a limited participation of the layman in the Church's ruling office. In the early Church, laymen participated in the selection of popes and bishops and sat in Church councils.

The layman is a ruler in his visible kingdom, which is creation. This was enjoined upon him by God who directed him to subdue the earth. In the present generation, man is spending his energy to bring space under his dominion with his Sputniks, Vanguards and interplanetary missiles. The layman as a member of the Mystical Body and a ruler of this world must exercise his kingship over things and people in conformity with Christ's justice and love, which is another way to say that he must "restore all things in Christ," or "bring all things to a head in Christ."

The layman shares in the priesthood of Christ through his

Baptism. He is a member of "a chosen race, a royal priest-hood." Pius XII in both *Mystici Corporis* and *Mediator Dei* did more than set limits to theological discussion; it encouraged us to share this truth of Christ's link with the laity through participation in His priesthood.

There is only one person in a diocese who holds the office of official teacher of the Church: the bishop. Priests in turn are collaborators of the bishop and by his delegation they speak for the Church. Yet laymen are urged to take their place in the apostolate of the Church, which is another name for the mission of the Church. It is the mission of the Church to teach or evangelize. The priestly dignity of the laity urged St. Peter Damian to encourage laymen to "announce the virtue of Christ to the world." In the train of Luther came the self-anointed preachers of the Word, with the result that the Council of Trent had to apply the brakes. Now that the siege is over, recent popes have been calling laymen to a more intimate cooperation with the official teachers of the faith. Popes have been encouraging mutual instruction by laymen in organized apostolates. General hierarchical mandates are given in order that laymen might legitimately assume teaching responsibilities in the Church.

Beyond the organized and approved apostolates of the Church, the ordinary day-to-day contacts of lay people with lay people demand a certain amount of witnessing or teaching in a wide sense, for which no mandate is needed. The power is given at Confirmation by the Holy Spirit "who gives us what to speak in that hour." Is the teaching mission of the Church involved when Joe Doakes sips a short beer with a friend on the way home from work, or Mrs. Jones discusses weighty problems over the back fence or a bridge table, or Mary Brown exchanges notes with the girls during a coffee break? Fellow-workers, our neighbors, marriage, love, birth control, and the

like are subjects that are discussed in these places. Cannot lay
Catholics participate in the tradition of prophetic utterance and
be authentic witnesses of Christ in these situations? This type
of apostolate seems to be a legitimate extension of the teaching
role of Christ and the Church. It would seem a bit undignified
for a bishop or pastor to fulfill his office personally in these circumstances, nor would he be as effective as one who "belongs."
Somehow, we have narrowed the teaching role of the Church to
the pulpit and the Catholic school and press. Yet only a minority of the world's population will ever sit before a Catholic
pulpit or in a Catholic school classroom or read a Catholic publication.

The Mystical Body channels the God-life to man through the
sacraments. The sacraments must be presented, not as mechani-
cal things that work automatically, but as contacts with Christ
in which He gives life initially, then strengthens it or restores it
through His divine mercy. Baptism must be taught not simply in
terms of the blotting out of sin, but also as an etching of the
priesthood of Christ upon the soul (the imprinting of the baptismal "character") and the giving of the array of virtues and
gifts, along with the indwelling of the Holy Spirit. Confirmation
is not only directly related to, but is the base of, the apostolate.
It is a social sacrament which implies a giving, unlike Baptism
which is more a receiving. It is given for the upbuilding of the
Body. It is thought of in terms of militancy. If we think of
militancy in terms of polemics and defending the ramparts of
the ghetto, we have a shockingly narrow view of Confirmation.
The sacrament is to mature us as witnesses for Christ as much
by service for our neighbor in the countless contacts of the day
as by martyrdom.

The chief support and source of the apostolate is the Mass.
Since the Mystical Body and divine life for men stem from

Christ's death, in this sense the Mass is primary since it re-presents Christ's death and resurrection. The Mass keeps worship and work in perspective. Man can link his work or service with the Mass and make his life a continuous going to the Father through Christ. This creates and deepens apostolic life. The Mass is the source of unity for the apostle, since it is corporate in its nature and effects. "Because the Bread is one," it establishes tighter bonds with our neighbor. There will be no apostolate of consequence without deep roots in the Mass.

Daily Mass with communion should be the goal for people interested in leading the full Catholic life, but this must be urged only within the context of what is possible. Distance to the church, small children at home, other children to prepare for school, the need of a reasonable amount of sleep, are reasons for not participating in Mass daily. These reasons should be accepted as valid, but they often do not apply to Saturday Mass. Once the latter is tried, daily Mass becomes an attainable goal for many who previously could not manage it.

No summary, however brief, of the theological truths upon which the apostolate is based is complete without establishing a place for Mary. If an apostle is to be formed in Christ, it will be through Mary. Mary has been established as not only the Mother of the physical Christ, but likewise as Mother of the Mystical Christ. Christ has associated Himself with her in the work of redemption to the point that she is fittingly called the Co-Redemptrix of the human race. Lay apostles will labor in vain unless the work is under the banner of the Queen of Apostles.

These are the necessary truths or doctrinal framework for the apostle. The next question is, how can these truths be best taught to people who are already engaged in a fulltime life pursuit? Schools of theology for the laity are springing up here and there which mark a great maturity and development from the catechetical approach for beginners. Such schools, if they are to be fruitful, must have students with an academic background or an intellectual curiosity. For the great mass of people who have lived on a steady diet of digests and escape literature, and for whom a meaty theological book would be considered an unmanageable aggressor, there must be another approach. The great truths of the divine life and the Mystical Body were not designed for an intellectual elite. They were first preached to the fishermen of Palestine and the stevedores of Corinth, and presented to them in the context of life.

We must re-think our approaches to these subjects. The small-group movements have already made a start. Members of The Legion of Mary use part of their meeting to come to a better understanding of Mariology. The Sodalists, too, use part of their meeting for doctrinal purposes. CFM, YCW, and YCS have in their meetings a ten-minute period devoted to what is mis-called "liturgy." Liturgy is really an *action* of the Church, not a discussion. In this part of the meeting they discuss the Mystical Body, the divine life, or some aspect of the liturgy, such as the liturgical year or the sacraments. Strictly speaking, it could not be justified as a part of a Catholic Action meeting if the teaching through the pulpit and classrooms were orientated toward the subject of divine life. It is filling a gap in religious education.

The American economy makes it possible for more people each year to leave home to make a closed retreat. The retreat movement in this country can be a great boon to the apostolate in proportion to its understanding of the needs of the apostolic layman. The week-end retreat for couples is the ideal for families. Both partners can hear the same truths together and work out their application after the retreat is over. During a week-end retreat, the great apostolic truths on which the apostolate is based are presented not as theses to be proved, but in a vital context and in an atmosphere of prayerful silence where deep convictions are formed. Days and evenings of recollection are substitutes for retreats, but necessary and effective substitutes. In fact, given the conditions of modern life and the number of people now actively engaged in the apostolate, closed retreats can hardly be a practical ideal. Frequent days or evenings of recollection should be provided as normal events throughout the year.

The hustle and bustle of city life has its way of destroying the prayer life of practising Catholics. The logical place to begin prayer is with the morning offering. At the right moment people should be introduced to meditation or mental prayer. The aim must be for simplicity, no involved formulas. The process must be seen as a loving conversation with God. Lay people have to devise means of working this into a busy life. Public transportation or driving to or from work, or the time from the end of Mass to breakfast might be utilized in creating this dialogue. On first thought, we might absolve the layman from any attempt to set aside time for meditation, but if sufficient conviction is generated everyone can discipline himself to finding ten minutes every day to commune with God. The parish itself, through days of recollection, annual retreats, and the impact of the major liturgical fasts and feasts, should take care of the longer periods which we need for seeing the overall picture of our life in God.

Reading is not prayer, but as a pump primer it is a powerful ally. Given the distracting conditions of life we often need the stimulus of a book to set our prayer in action. We need books like Howell's *Of Sacrifice and Sacraments* to ground us in the liturgy. Ultimately, the scriptures must be tasted and digested.

The liturgy itself has been too long overlooked as the great teacher in the Church. In the early Church this was the chief means of teaching. The liturgy brings the Bible and tradition together in a living unity. The missal is the Church's best religion textbook. The intelligent celebration of a single feast, the Easter vigil, weaves together the array of doctrines needed for the apostolate: Baptism, the waters of divine grace, fellowship in the Mystical Body through vocal participation, offering and sharing in the Paschal Lamb. To a lesser degree, this is true of all the feasts of the Church year. The most brilliant theological lectures can supplement, but never substitute, for this type of learning in which the emotions as well as the mind are caught up in the incense of praise to the Father.

The liturgy covers all truths but without the scientific order of the textbook and the props of the classroom. It teaches through repetition, the mother of learning. The recurring annual cycle of feasts and fasts never permits our learning to be a dead letter. This method of learning allows for family participation and improvisation through para-liturgical ceremonies on the pastor's part, and liturgical customs in the home. Families may introduce readings, prayers and symbols that keep the redemption theme alive and growing. People may be unaccustomed to family reading, but not to symbols. People regulate their lives by symbols, but the trouble is that the symbols of success, such as the Cadillac, the ranch-style home, Calvert's, chrome finish, and the rest are all non-sacred signs, leading to dead-end streets and the psychiatrist's couch. The sacred signs that have their roots in Jewish history and Christian antiquity, and which keep before us the message of our redemption, have lost their meaning with the centuries. As the liturgy comes to life again in the twentieth century, new symbols will be found to remind us of old truths.

In recent years the Liturgical Press and other presses have been turning out an increasing volume of literature that services the Catholic home. Grailville has long been in the field encouraging family customs that help us grasp religious mysteries. The National Catholic Council of Women on a national level and, in particular, in dioceses such as Cincinnati and San Francisco, is continuously addressing itself to these practical problems.

What norms should guide families in the selection and adaptation of these customs? The approach should be a very gradual and realistic one. The cook-book approach to the liturgy is probably a poor way to introduce it to others, just as too many liturgical designs might be the best way of losing our friends and neighborly contacts. People should not be asked to pay a price for our friendship because we are interested in liturgical art. Yet we cannot submit to sterile conformity, nor can we, in the words of Bloy, "suffocate luminous souls in the sentimental slime of a stupid piety, which is the most monstrous form of the corruption of the innocent." A few prints or symbols well placed and occasionally changed might be a good compromise.

The danger of people becoming preoccupied with liturgical customs is the danger of anyone getting engrossed in anything to the point of losing a sensitivity to other important aspects of life, such as neighborhood concerns and our wider relationships with society and social problems. A young philosophy professor and father of a family expressed it thus: "I have myself known families, who in their desire to sanctify their lives, to become more perfect Christians, have conceived that in order to sanctify their marriage, it was necessary to turn the home into a kind of little monastery, where prayers were recited at regular hours during the day. Naturally, such couples tended to become more withdrawn from the neighborhood in which they lived than a family in which prayers were fitted to the ordinary routine of life; e.g., grace before meals, a family rosary, but not multiplication of prayers at odd hours. I am not, of course, deprecating the power of prayer, but merely suggesting that the apostolate is not primarily one of prayer, but of action."

We are not presenting contrary ideas: the family with a liturgical prayer life opposed to the family that is dedicated to the apostolate. There is nothing irreconcilable about the family using occasional psalms for prayers, the father reading aloud passages from the Bible, the whole family preparing for and celebrating feasts with prayers and designs, and at the same time both parents devoting much time to the apostolate outside the family circle. We are merely establishing a hierarchy. The apostolate needs the help of a rich and meaningful prayer life to make it fruitful. The family filled with the vision and the beauty and peace which the liturgy gives needs the demands of the apostolate to keep the liturgy from becoming a fetish. We are simply trying to establish a balance between the liturgical life of the family and the missionary role of the family.

Catholic Action and the lay apostolate are pressing theologians to reconsider the relationship of prayer and action. The ideal of Mary as the contemplative, in contrast to Martha as the activist, has made it seem impossible for the person who has a large family or a demanding position in secular life to live the Christian life to the full.

One could line up a list of quotations from celebrated authors that would discourage one from action. St. Bernard refers to works that dissipate us interiorly as "accursed works." Action can disperse us, impassion us. It can be a source of pride and tumble our spiritual edifice like a house of cards. Thomas à Kempis reminds us that "they who go abroad much are rarely sanctified." Dom Chautard's classic, *The Soul of the Apostolate,*

with all the warnings against the loss of the interior life, hardly
encourages us to action.

Apostolic action must be viewed positively as a source of
sanctity. It can no longer be viewed as a rival to contemplation.
Both contemplation and apostolic action have the same end,
which is God. They are both motivated by the love of God, and,
therefore, are two aspects of charity. Growth in charity means
that actions become infused with a contemplative spirit, that is,
one finds Christ in the action or the recipient of the action.
Also, it means that the love of God in daily life compels us to
express it in action.

The layman and the diocesan priest are already immersed in
action. They have no choice as Christians but to purify the action, and thus infuse into it the contemplative spirit. It seems
unreal to ask people to cease acting and not to show them
that, ordinarily, what they are doing is the will of God and
basically is an active love which is capable of greater intensity
through further purification of the dross of selfishness or impa-
tience. Action is soil for love. Growth in love of God blossoms
from fraternal charity. We have a divine source of fraternal
charity in the Eucharist, the sacrament of love. Divinizing action demands a closer link between Mass and daily life. Lay
people involved in the apostolate must be brought to appreciate
this link.

St. Augustine is a realist when he says: "The love of God is
the first commandment; but by beginning with the second, one
comes to the first. If you do not love your neighbor whom you
see, how can you love God whom you do not see?" Contemplation in the real order follows action. Most people will discover
God in action. It will be the ordinary way they will touch God.
Christ will reveal Himself to them as He did to His disciples on
the road to Emmaus in the breaking of the bread, which can be

a symbol for any action on behalf of our fellow men. It is conceivable that the priest and Levite on the road from Jerusalem to Jericho were reciting the psalms of David as Catholic priests do when they travel. They may have been so engrossed in their psalms that they failed to recognize in their distressed brother the One who inspired the psalms. Contemplation and action are not rivals, but must be fused and together form an act of love.

The emphasis on the Mystical Body, participation of the laity in the Mass, and the incarnation of the Church in society, express themselves today in new forms. In church architecture, we have compact naves close to the altar, where clergy and laity are able to perform their functions as a unit. In theology we have change, too. Times demand not new doctrines, but an emphasis on the doctrines especially needed in our particular historical circumstances. Divine Life, the Mystical Body, the kingship of Christ, the full liturgical life, and charity in action are capable of further exploration in our times. A beginning has been made.

CHAPTER XII

The Priesthood Amidst Change

Priests are not notorious for their collections of relics and religious articles, but it is not uncommon to find in the bedroom of one a relic of St. John Vianney, better known as the Curé of Ars. The outline of his life is familiar to every priest. He was born in an obscure French village in the eighteenth century. His name is associated with constant failures in his studies during his seminary days and genuine holiness of life. Ordained a priest because of an acute shortage of vocations, he was sent to the rural district of Ars in 1818 to take over a parish of some 300 people. The faith and morality of Ars had declined to the point that blasphemy was common and Sunday Mass was neglected for little reason. It was the Curé's intense prayer life and austere fasting that proved to be his decisive weapons in wrestling with the devil.

In certain cases, our Blessed Lord tells us, prayer and fast-

ing are our only weapons; ordinarily, they are both used as
part of the priest's pastoral ministry. Without discounting these
indispensable aids, which are valid for every generation, I
would like to consider the Curé's actual pastoral work. His pastoral approach was a direct one. With a total of sixty households in his parish, he needed no convent of sisters to teach the
children; he taught the catechism lessons himself. He needed no
Legion of Mary members or other lay helpers to make frequent
visits to the negligent Catholics. There was no need of IBM or
multi-colored census cards; he could carry a day-to-day progress report of each parishioner in his head.

The Curé preached for an hour on Sunday; there was no
problem of hourly Masses without adequate parking facilities in
the area. The current evils, as he saw them, were drinking,
dancing and immodest dress. By sheer force of his spiritual
leadership and his direct approach with the saloon keepers, he
was able to close the four taverns in Ars. His denial of abso-
lution in the confessional was effective in stopping dances. Since
the majority of his people were illiterate and the mass media
communications were still unknown, there were no outside in-
fluences undermining his sway over their minds. Ars had one
voice—his.

If an urban priest confines his ministry to the pulpit, the confessional, parish visits, and the teaching of catechism, how effective will he be? He does well to average seven minutes in the
pulpit on Sunday exclusive of announcements, letters, and appeals. Since people can shop around for the kind of confessor
they want, the confessional provides no effective control over
his flock. If he attempted to close a movie house for showing
an indecent picture, he would probably fail or drive the business
to a more distant theatre. While the peasant could spend the
week reflecting on Sunday's sermon, the priest's voice today

is vying with the evening news telecaster, the syndicated columnists, the heads of trade associations, the union and political party leaders and a host of lesser pundits.

The big city parish almost defies the systematic visiting of homes. At best the priest can recognize names and addresses of parishioners. The tendency then is to visit no one unless an urgent problem is brought to light which requires the attention of a priest. The priest today knows that the chief evils of society are not drinking, dancing, and immodest dress. He may not be able to give a sociological analysis but he knows that today there are subtler evils which go by such vague names as materialism and secularism.

What these facts reveal is a perennial problem, namely adapting, not the priesthood as a sacrament, but its pastoral expression in the concrete circumstances of history and geography. This is an unending process. Social workers are continually exploring new problems or new facets of old ones without having satisfactorily resolved previous ones. Only the novice thinks that social problems are neatly and permanently solved like algebraic equations.

So it is with the priesthood in a changing world. The priest must be constantly involved in the process of adaptation and adjustment as the normal everyday concern of his ministry. In the tradition-bound agrarian society of eighteenth-century rural France, fidelity to existing patterns made for stability, and in Ars for holiness. In a dynamic industrial society fidelity to structures that were designed to solve problems or meet needs of another century puts one in the category of the horse and buggy or the dinosaur. In the priesthood, as in any other way of life, we must always be engaged in examining the status quo. When the process stops, rigor mortis sets in for the parish and the priest.

One way to study change in the role of the priest is to contrast the attitudes of two recent popes, St. Pius X and Pius XII, in their encyclicals on the priesthood. From a cursory reading of both encyclicals, one might say that their only differences were in expression and emphasis, since both cover the usual topics of a priest's retreat: meditation, spiritual reading, examination of conscience, priestly charity and the like.

A more careful reading of the two texts would dissipate such a superficial observation. One indication of a difference in approach can be found in a somewhat chance expression of St. Pius X. He uses the phrase "filth of this world" when he is admonishing priests about worldly reading. One would have to search the thousands of pages of Pius XII's writings to find such an expression. Pius XII was fully aware of the power of the Prince of Darkness and the trail of evil he leaves as he goes about seeking whom he may devour, but the late pope seemed more impressed with a world that is full of wonder, the many-faceted creation destined to be brought under the enriching influence of Christ's redemptive power. He continually addressed groups from foundry men to gymnasts, people from all walks of life. He did not talk to them with a simple religious vocabulary about their soul, but rather he tried to elaborate the great contribution they could make through their work, profession, or recreation to humanizing the world so that it may become a fitting receptacle of the divine.

There are even more obvious differences in the encyclicals. Under the heading of charity, St. Pius includes the teaching of catechism, the defense and exposition of the Church and the missionary apostolate. Pius XII adds to charity another dimension with a section, entitled "Current Problems," in which he writes about the abuses of the economic system and urges "priests to remain faithful to the social teaching of the Church and to spread the knowledge of it." He adds, "This teaching unites and perfects the demands of justice and the duties of charity."

The importance of lay people in the apostolate was recognized by St. Pius X, but not mentioned in his encyclical on the priesthood. With Pius XII, the training of lay people is part of the priesthood and thus is incorporated into his encyclical. "Ordinarily, the carrying out of these Christian social principles in public life is the task of the laity, but where no capable lay Catholics are found, the priest should make every effort to train some adequately."

The development in the role of the priesthood which is reflected in these encyclicals is the result of historical circumstances. St. Pius X was struggling against the errors of Modernism within the household of the faith. He had to close ranks, thus his role to a great extent was a defensive one. Pius XII came to the papacy after Modernism had become history and the Lateran Treaty had given the Church status and acceptance with the rulers of this world. Since Piux XII inherited an orderly household and a less hostile world, he could devote his energies to making advances into the world that he, as Christ's vicar, was commissioned to bring redemption to.

History books are filled with sad lessons of good men who did not understand their times. Leo XIII, for example, pleaded with French Catholics to forget about reviving the monarchy and to make peace with the Republic. Leo was a hard-bitten realist who realized that the Republic had to be accepted, like a bride, for better or worse, and the days of monarchy and privilege had to be forgotten. But he could not force his view. He could only warn, and then sit back and watch the folly of futile rear-guard actions. The time lag between papal pronouncements and their practical acceptance always damages

the Mystical Body. We have been familiar with the obvious
tragedies of the priesthood, since the evening when Judas rose
from the table and turned his back on our Lord. There is another kind of tragedy, not at all obvious, which is a triumph,
nevertheless, for the Prince of Darkness. This is for a devout
priest stationed in a twentieth century urban parish to exercise
his ministry according to the demands of a rural, nineteenth
century parish. Today's priest has a compelling need to study
social change in the ministry of the eternal priesthood.

The priestly role today

"The office proper to a priest," writes St. Thomas, "is to be
a mediator between God and the people. . . ." Christ is the
mediator between God and man. He became mediator in the
womb of Mary by virtue of the union of the divine and human
natures in one person. By becoming a man, the Second Person
of the Blessed Trinity became a member of the human race.
This fact of being one of us made Him a mediator. Thus, He
could take upon Himself the sins of the human race. While ex-
empt from sin He was a member of a fallen race. On the cross
He achieved its restoration. On the cross His mediation or His
priesthood reached its climax. He exercised His priesthood to
its fullness in offering Himself to His Father.

Each ordained priest participates in Christ's priesthood to
the point that he renews the redemptive work of Christ as often
as he offers holy Mass. Lay people, because of their Baptism,
share the priesthood of Christ. However, their exercise of this
common priesthood at Mass depends upon the priesthood of
Holy Orders. The priest, then, is the ordinary channel through
which Christ's life comes to lay people, who in the words of St.
Peter are "a chosen race, a royal priesthood, a holy nation, a
purchased people."

The first duty, then of both priest and people is to worship. The sacrament of Holy Orders gives the priest the power from God to act as the representative of the whole Church, and particularly of the baptized members who come to offer sacrifice with him. Flowing from the priest's role of offering sacrifice is the duty to pray for God's people and administer the sacraments. All these functions take priority over his role in the temporal order. Although these essentially priestly roles are the most important ones, his role in the temporal order is not unrelated to his priesthood or unimportant. Cardinal Suhard, writing for priests, said: "Take careful note of this. The salvation of persons cannot be accomplished without a certain salvation of the social order. . . . A priest will fail in his vocation if he confines his effort to the salvation of persons, for he has not only souls for parishioners, but problems, organizations, and a given section of space and time in the city of this world." However, as a priest he does not take his place in the temporal order as the layman, who has the primary responsibility for it. The priest must carry out the prophetic tradition of being God's mouthpiece. It is not enough for him to help lay people take their part in lay life. He has his own witness to bear in society. He does this by speaking out whenever the dignity of man is affronted by certain pieces of legislation or by the lack of certain legislative measures, when the government takes away man's freedom by doing too much, or leaves him in his misery by not doing what man unaided cannot do. For this witness-bearing, the priest must expect to be rebuked and misunderstood.

The priest must also understand the possible bad effects of his playing the role of an Isaias or an Amos and destroying the false idols. In speaking out forthrightly against the evils of the day, or taking a stand on controversial issues, he finds himself cast in the role of savior of the people. Lay people can be fascinated by the priest's rhetorical triumphs and polemic skills to the point that they feel no need to investigate the issues, study the problem or assume responsibility for effective action. Lay people become partisans like the bleacher fans in the ball park. They identify themselves with the cause but as spectators. Unfortunately, the right-field bleacher fan is less capable of playing right field after twenty years of bleacher sitting than he was when he first identified himself with the team. The contribution of many lay people amounts to cheering the priest on to doing the work of Catholic Action. It is a very satisfying feeling for lay people to turn the TV dial to a program where a cleric is either expounding Catholic doctrine or exposing a modern error. When the program is finished the viewer feels he has done something.

Besides inhibiting the laity, the priest's oratorical brilliance and personal success can blind him to certain aspects of his own vocation. He can become indifferent to the value of the long-term and often discouraging work of helping people develop themselves as competent leaders and fully developed Christians. The direct witness of the priest, wherein he plays a leadership role, conflicts with, at times, and even prevents the witnessing that should be done by lay people. There is no rule of thumb to tell a priest whether he should attend a city council meeting when a civil rights issue is at stake, or sit through a small-group meeting where his contribution will be less spectacular and less rewarding in terms of immediate accomplishments.

The modern Amos must work through committees to destroy modern idols. Meetings demand listening more than talking. The priest who is keenly aware of his commission through ordination to preach, teach, and thus carry on the prophetic tradition of being minister of the Word feels a tension in his life when he plays the role of listener. He squirms and fidgets when he abstains from discussion wherein lay people are laboriously and circuitously formulating doctrinal answers which he could give them quickly and with precise theological phraseology. Experience should teach him that people learn best when they can think out loud and when the expert does not choke the learning process by handing out the answers before the problem is probed.

There will be little accomplished in the Church by lay people unless they understand the part the priest has to play in their spiritual development. They must learn to expect more from the priest than that he start Mass on time and be available for Baptisms, marriages, sick calls and funerals. They must understand that he has something they need for full Christian living and without which they ordinarily cannot reach their full stature. He has something to give that even the best-educated lay Catholic cannot do without. It is the priest's job to help form Christ in the Christian. Lay people can discuss a gospel selection together, or study the liturgy or Catholic social doctrine together, but very often in applying this to their lives they need priestly counsel. This is not simply because the priest has read learned books on counselling, but because Christ has given him this power to help.

A young lady expressed a mature view of what to expect from a priest. She expressed herself thus: "It has always been my conviction that the work of the priest is to help us become active, mature Christians. One of the ways this is done is by having priests skilled enough to guide us along the lines of thinking things out for ourselves—that is, thinking straight for ourselves. This in itself is not an easy task. With every sort of pressure acting on young people from TV to advertising, it takes a great deal of skill and patience to make them think things out for themselves, make good judgments, and feel the conviction for action and the determination to carry it through. It would be so much easier for the priest to just tell us what the answers are instead of sitting quietly at our meetings while the kids go 'round and 'round. This point of thinking for oneself seems very important to me, if we are ever to have mature Christians. Too often we come across people who are either rectory parasites—running to the priest for every trivial thing because they are not capable of making proper decisions for themselves—or people who resent the 'authoritarian attitude' of the Church in regard to marriage, social problems and so forth, because they are too far away from the Church and its thinking to really understand."

The modern priest-prophet needs to be a man with burning convictions, but his manner of presentation needs to fit his times and his audience. To help develop an articulate laity, he must learn the art of creative silence.

Listening is a way of paying respect to others. It demands abandonment of one's pet remedies in order to pursue the other person's ideas. If one wishes to understand people, he must hear them express themselves in their own idiom. This sensitivity to reality finds its way back to the people in sermons, talks, and private counselling sessions, and thus creates an empathy with those who listen to the good listener now speaking. When this relationship is established, a fertile ground has been prepared for sowing the Word.

Silence is demanded of the priest not only in meetings but even in the confessional. The confessional can be used to give little homilies, varying with the sin or the season, to unknown penitents—a procedure which could be accomplished just as well by a recording system wherein the confessor would press the button for anger, missing Mass, or neglecting one's Easter duty. Often, while talking, the priest is blissfully unaware that the relieved penitent, his sins confessed, is politely but impatiently waiting for the sign to go. A better understanding of human nature might lead the priest to involve the person in a searching self-examination by a question that demanded a thoughtful answer. A fruitful dialogue could thus be started. Our Lord dealt this way with the woman he met at the well of Jacob. He engaged her in a conversation about well water, and then brought the dialogue to a consideration of living water or divine life. The conversation changed the woman from an adulteress to an apostle. She went from the well to the town to tell others of the prophet.

If lay people are ever to assume their rightful place in the Church, it will be the result of priests assisting them as chaplains of apostolic groups, as confessors and spiritual counselors. The work of forming Christ in souls and preparing lay people for the apostolate is less glamorous, more trying and exacting, and demands greater skills than preaching, teaching, or personally witnessing to Christ in the social arena. It is called by St. Gregory the Great "the art of arts."

The key to successful spiritual guidance lies in the priest's understanding of the layman's life and aspirations—not just the layman in general but this particular person with his unique personality and history. To simply prescribe more frequent use of the Eucharist and Penance is not going to change the people who will change the world. "Frequent the sacraments and resist temptations" is too platitudinous to be helpful. Spiritual direction, to be useful and productive, must result from a relationship that is built on a sympathetic understanding of the circumstances of life of the person seeking counsel.

Spiritual help is often best given by indirection, especially in the beginning, when people are unaware that they should be seeking it or have no knowledge of how they should get it. Priests find that to help people give speeches, lead meetings, or plan an activity, creates an excellent opportunity for either party to lead the discussion into an application of the speech, the meeting or the activity, to the person's own life. Since the subject under discussion is not pointedly directed at the person, there is no embarrassment on either side if the lay person does not catch the implications the priest is subtly pointing out. The common endeavor gives both sides the opportunity to speak freely about matters that either would be reluctant to broach directly.

The great advantage for both layman and priest in their involvement in apostolic groups is that some of the items suggested under the heading of spiritual direction are woven into meetings: prayer is discussed, Mass is encouraged, bibliographies of spiritual books are included in the manuals. A relationship is built up between priest and group members which helps the members in approaching the priest privately for special help.

Out of this involvement of people and laity on a spiritual level, there is developing a new relationship between priest and people. This is positively disturbing to older priests who believe that respect for the cloth can be best maintained by a rigid formality. They believe in kindness, courtesy, and service, but never in an association that has spontaneity and warmth. They have seen curates become attached to families to the point of neglecting their work and setting up an aristocracy within the parish. This view deserves a hearing and stands as a warning of what can happen to well-intentioned but unregulated friendships with the laity.

The corroding influence of clerical inflexibility needs no illustration. This attitude may result from a feeling of insecurity in the presence of a laity who are better educated and have more *savoir faire* than the priest. The cloth can be used to shield real or imagined deficiencies. In defense of what might be considered as an aggressive laity, the priest may try to reinforce his position through the use of authoritarian methods. Still, he cannot stop the clock when personal relationships are changing in other segments of life; the authoritarian approach will only bring him the despair and pity of his flock.

The new relationship that is dawning is not born of an anti-clerical spirit. On the contrary, it manifests a genuine reverence for the priesthood and an awareness of the priest's necessary limitations as an administrator, financier, architect, scholar and educator. The laity realize that a spiritual father needs time for prayer and spiritual reading if his words are not to have an empty ring. They are willing to share with him the responsibility for which they have a capability, on one condition. The priest must trust the judgment of the one to whom he assigns responsibility and thus permit him to use his head as well as his hands. The business world in which the layman is immersed is organized; it works through committees and delegates power. Lay people acting in voluntary relationships expect their pastor to play the role of chairman of the board or senior partner, not dictator or "boss man."

When there is this interplay between priest and people there is no fear of encroaching upon someone's rights. On the contrary, where we have lay organizations in which the chaplain is a mere functionary, appearing only to give invocations or an occasional talk, there is real danger of a wall of separation and a consequent anti-clericalism.

The priest as lord of all he surveys is a European tradition that is as out of place in the American scene as wooden shoes and the Dutch windmill. Today there are many signs of a more human relationship between priests and people in this country. For example, segregation patterns in seating arrangements of priest and laity are becoming extinct. In Washington, D. C., the couple who leads the monthly Cana meeting invites the chaplain to their home for dinner prior to the meeting, to prepare for it. This easy approach sets the climate for lasting commitment on the part of the lay people. The very novelty of having a priest to dinner caused a housewife to call another Cana wife and ask, "What do you feed a priest?"

Teamwork between priest and laity is based on their incorporation into one Body by Baptism. The teamwork is a "fellowship in Christ," or "fellowship in the Church." There is no need to fear that the hierarchic structure will suffer. This structure has been sufficiently strengthened and stressed since the Council of Trent, so much so that the Pauline expressions, "members one of another," "baptised into a single Body," "united in mind and judgment," are like refreshing zephyrs from another world, when applied to the lay-clerical relationship.

Teamwork between priest and laity is another way of creating a Christian community, and from this teamwork or community should come lay saints. Michael de la Bedoyere has a sentence worth underlining: "The saint springs from the fellowship of the Church . . . consider the history of the great religious orders . . . and the fellowship of the Church is the school for saints." Our age should bring to the Church "Mr. and Mrs." saints, lawyer saints, worker saints, etc.

If the seminary has not prepared the priest for these many facets of the ministry, how can he acquire them? Or if it has, how can he nurture them? When a young priest discovers through experience that lay people grow in Christ through group action, he asks himself why this fruitful group experience must be confined to lay folk. As a result of experience with Catholic Action groups, priests' groups have been formed. There are no distinct or clear-cut patterns for these meetings. Ordinarily, they are loosely organized without any intention of making the group permanent. The intention is not to form a structure that would perpetuate the group, but rather to meet informally but regularly as long as the group finds it profitable. No two groups have the same content to their meetings. Some begin with a discussion on a papal encyclical that might have special relevance to the priestly ministry itself, such as an encyclical on the priesthood or the liturgy. Others might begin with a discussion on the Mass or prayer. Often priests find this the first time in their priesthood that they could discuss their difficulties in prayer with someone other than their confessor. This frank discussion of personal and pastoral difficulties with sympathetic brethren creates the same solidarity and mutual support that lay people experience from discussions on a passage of the Gospel.

If the layman by Confirmation is commissioned to bring the fruits of Christianity to others—what we call the apostolate— the priest through the sacrament of Holy Orders is similarly, and even more dramatically, commissioned. When the priest sees lay people searching their own lives, through the social inquiry, in an effort to bear witness there, he too wonders why he cannot discuss the aspects of the priestly apostolate with his fellow-priests.

If the first part of these clerical meetings deals with personal problems, it is natural for the second part to consist of a lengthy discussion of an aspect of the priestly apostolate. This section may cover a wide variety of subjects such as visiting the sick, retrieving lapsed Catholics, giving spiritual direction to apostolic lay people, or racial segregation.

Like lay people, priests need mutual encouragement. They

need to establish deeper and more meaningful ties than those formed by the ordinary clerical forms of recreation. There are groups of priests who take summer vacations together in order to have prolonged discussions on the apostolate, interlarded with fishing, golf, and extra sleep. They come back to their parishes spiritually, intellectually, and physically refreshed and with tighter bonds of clerical friendships.

Other priests prefer to tie a convention or two into their vacation. Seldom do bishops and pastors allow curates time for conventions. The groups of priests who travel to the annual Liturgical Week or to the study week of an apostolic movement such as the Young Christian Workers usually do so at their own expense and time. This gives to the meetings a seriousness, depth, and spontaneity that is often lacking in diocesan-sponsored clerical conferences. There is a spirit created at these national meetings, where priests from opposite ends of the country meet, that could not be captured from a local get-together.

As much as we need national meetings for specialized fields of the apostolate, we need in every diocese a team or teams of priests who are specialists or have a special competence in a particular field. The sum of knowledge the modern priest needs in our complex society cannot possibly be achieved through personal experience or private study alone. While the parish priest must always remain the general practitioner, he can, in a limited way, through his natural talents or his reading manage to make a distinctive contribution to his fellow-priests. Great changes can take place in a diocese where the best minds meet with some regularity over a decade or two. Talents which might otherwise be wasted are nurtured and rendered useful in this group situation. The priest-team is the most efficient means of communicating and discussing the latest developments in pastoral approaches. No one questions the need for specialists. The difficulty is in the line of communication between the specialist and the practitioner who must apply the specialist's conclusions if they are to have their effect.

The priest as a professional man can be absorbed in how-to-do-it formulas and fail to develop himself intellectually and culturally. When a broad approach is lacking, the practical man is lost, and his neatly packaged plans no longer meet the situation. The parish priest, like the busy family doctor, can excuse himself from non-professional reading, but if he has a respect for learning he can manage to keep alive his interests by contacts with other priests and lay people who do read. Exchanging books, formal and informal discussions with priests and lay people who are capable of intellectual pursuits, can stimulate both priest and lay person and create the beginnings of an intellectual community. Without this community of interest, the pressure of routine work and the compulsive presence of the mass communication media in the rectory will stifle the pursuit of wisdom for wisdom's sake.

If there is to be a widespread change in the priest-layman relationship, the starting point would logically seem to be the seminary. Realistically, however, the seminary might be the last place for the change to be felt. The new clerical-lay relationship is being brought about by social changes that have their roots in the political and economic orders, areas which in this century and country belong to the layman. Geographically and culturally, the seminary is further removed from these areas than the parish rectory or the Catholic school.

This condition has resulted from Church policy. Previous to the Council of Trent, there was no seminary other than the bishop's house, the monastery, or the university. This loose arrangement resulted in a clergy that to a shocking degree was unlearned and undisciplined. The Council tightened the reins on the clergy by setting up a separate institution for their education called a seminary. This institution was a combination of a university and a monastery without being either. The result was a clergy that has a professional knowledge of its vocation and a degree of discipline that did not exist previously in the history of the Church. The price for this achievement was loss of contact with the university world and the problems of lay life.

Pius XII, in *Menti Nostrae* and *Sedes Sapientiae,* faced this dilemma squarely. He wanted to close the gap between seminary and lay life without forfeiting the benefits of the closed community. This places a heavy burden on seminary faculties; without sacrificing the basic content of the seminary course, which is outlined in detail by the Holy See, teachers must adapt it to the needs of the modern priest. For the seminary professor who understands his role in the Church today, a tension will be created. He must pursue his intellectual and scholarly interests and yet keep close to the currents of lay life. He must live in a quasi-monastic enclosure and make his own the aspirations of the man on the street.

One means of accomplishing this aim in the seminary would be to establish rapport with lay people on a professional basis. Lay people could be brought to the seminary as special lecturers on subjects in which they have competence and which are related to specific seminary courses. The social order, marriage, counselling, education, public speaking, are some of the subjects in which the lay and clerical fields of endeavor overlap. Contact with lay people who are heroically devoting their spare time to lay apostolic work can give the seminary professor and his students insight into the spiritual problems of people who are trying to live the counsels of perfection in the midst of a welter of family, economic, and apostolic problems. If it would seem strange to teach medicine with straight lecture methods and never see, much less work on, a cadaver, it must be equally strange for a seminary which is preparing spiritual directors for laymen never to hear a layman state his difficulties in order that the class might dissect them and prescribe remedies.

The current religious revival in secular colleges and universities should challenge seminary professors to meet on common ground with their intellectual peers in secular and sectarian schools. Beginnings have been made. For example, the discovery of the Dead Sea scrolls has helped build a bridge between Catholic and Protestant scripture scholars. There will be a place in the Church for the theological polemicist, as long as organizations like the PAOU exist, but the pressing need of our times is for the theologian with the irenic approach. Until the seminary adjusts itself to the needs of the day, within and without the household of the faith, there will be a cultural lag in the Church's confrontation of the modern world.

While the priest's life is to be all things to all men, he has a hierarchy of values to observe in his actions. His first task is the liturgy. At the altar he is the mediator *par excellence* between God and man. He ministers Christ not only by distributing the Bread of Life, but also by dispensing the Word in and out of the pulpit and the confessional, in and out of meetings of all kinds. With limited time and unlimited demands he must have convictions about the importance and urgency of the works within his competency. With a sense of history, he must perceive that the layman is responsible for the temporal order and that the priest, in turn, is to withdraw from the impossible task of trying by his presence to represent the Church everywhere. The compelling task of the priest in our generation is to furnish inspiration and spiritual guidance to the layman who is trying to find the implications of the Gospel in the temporal order. His great priestly role in our day is to help shape these people for the apostolate.

Pius XII was deeply concerned that priests give themselves to this work of assisting the Holy Spirit in the forming of Christ in lay people. In 1954, while too weak to speak to the pastors and Lenten preachers of Rome, he wrote out a message to them in long hand, despite his illness and fatigue. In this message he said:

> But, above all, take care of their spiritual formation. Have them put on Jesus Christ; nourish them with Him, make of His Divine Heart a model from which they may draw inspiration in their thoughts, their affections, desires, words and actions. Have them surrender their heart in Jesus and in the arms of the heavenly Mother. . . . The apostolate must be exercised in factories, in schools, in large apartment houses, and not only by one's actions; there must be someone to initiate and bring into action, under your guidance and with your blessing, a band of "lay missionaries." Be exacting in pointing out their goals to them and be constant in encouraging them toward their realization . . . leave them sufficient scope for developing a spirit of eager and fruitful initiative. . . .

Thus another modern Pope has elaborated the teamwork that must be achieved by priests and layman in bringing the Mystical Body to its fullness. Lay people cannot do the job without having access to the treasures of divine life that the priest can open by reason of his priesthood. Likewise, the priest will accomplish little that is lasting if he does not help lay people find their place in the Church. The salvation of the human race does not rest with the priest or the laity alone but with the Church, which includes both. The late Cardinal Suhard states it thus: "The complete instrument of evangelization is neither the one who has simply been baptized nor the priest alone, but the Christian community."